Ruined by Design

How Designers Destroyed the World,
and What We Can Do to Fix It

Mike Monteiro

Editors: Ani King and Erika Hall
Proofreaders: Amanda Durbin and Mandy Keifetz
Indexer: Mandy Keifetz
Composition: Miguel Mosquito
Cover Design: Miguel Mosquito

Mule Books
601 Minnesota St. #122, SF, CA 94107

Last of the independents.

Contents

This book is dedicated to Bahtiyar Duysak, who, for eleven glorious minutes in 2017, deactivated Donald Trump's Twitter account.

Foreword

by Vivianne Castillo

In the early 1900s, some psychiatric hospitals gauged patients' readiness to integrate back into society through a simple and peculiar test. The patient was ushered into a room with a sink, where the hospital staff would place a plug in the sink, turn on the faucet, and wait for the sink to overflow. As water bubbled over the ledge and splashed onto the floor below, the patient was then handed a mop and the staff would leave the room, closing the door behind them. If the patient turned off the water, unplugged the sink, and mopped up the water that had spilled onto the floor, they were deemed as ready to go home and enter back into society. But if the patient opted to frantically mop as the water gushed over the sink, failing to turn off the faucet or remove the sink's plug, they were deemed insane and prescribed more time in the psychiatric hospital: they failed to acknowledge and address the root of the problem.

Many of you in the tech industry are frantically mopping.

You've said things, done things at your company that crushed your soul but paid your bills. You avoid talking to your friends and family about your company and ethics because, well, your company is always in the news for their lack of regard for people's privacy, data, and overall well-being. You've applied to companies who frequent news cycles for doing harm to others because you really want their name or a title on your resume. You want to laugh—then sob—at all the hypocritical, unethical design decisions you've witnessed, engaged in, or read—all under the banner of human-centered design, empathy or design thinking. You don't want to talk about politics and how it affects design, your job, your co-workers, and society. You don't understand why or how design is political nor do you care to engage that conversation. You've found yourself saying, "Well, I know that Project WTF is unethical and problematic... but that's not my team." You've started to feel cynical about the state of the tech industry, wondering if it'll ever get better.

You're frantically mopping, and haven't quite figured out how to address the waters you've waded into.

In this book, *Ruined by Design*, Mike Monteiro crafts an impressive and thorough commentary on the disturbing trends in the tech industry, provoking the reader to muse on their own complicity in harming others through skillful storytelling and the desire to do and be better. Each section thoughtfully evokes a sense of urgency—threaded together with rightful anger and ultrapractical hope—and provides space for the reader to grapple with the importance of community, professional organizations, and licensing.

If you've grown content and comfortable with the constant repackaging and selling of books that discuss best practices and how to more effectively implement [insert design agency name and their claim to fame for inventing a method or design process], then this book isn't for you.

But if you want to wade into the murky waters of the tech industry; if you're wanting to think more deeply about the power and ethical responsibility you have in this industry; if you're perplexed but not in despair; if you're ready to think about the direct impact our work has on the individuals and families exposed to the experiences and products you help create; if you're ready to turn off the faucet; rip the plug out of the sink, and put your mop to use—this book is for you.

Intro

We are so fucked. In fact, we are so fucked, it may already be too late for this book.

By the time you read this, Greenland may have melted, causing the world's oceans to rise by twenty feet. By the time you read this, everyone in the United States may be dead in a gunfight. By the time you read this, some idiot country may have launched a bomb at another idiot country. Facebook may have ~~accidentally~~ released everyone's private information into the public sphere, Twitter leadership may be getting measured for their new Hugo Boss uniforms, and Silicon Valley may be lobbying Congress to just make women illegal. In which case, nothing in this book will matter.

So the fact that I'm writing this book is either the most stupid or the most hopeful act I can imagine. To be honest with you, I think it's a bit of both.

Either way, all of the horrible things listed above may happen, or may not happen, but they're definitely within the realm of possibility. And they're within the realm of possibility because we didn't do what we could to stop it. More than that, it's possible because that's how we designed the world. We designed the combustion engine that led to global warming (climate change deniers can just stop reading right now). We designed the guns that kill school children. We designed shitty interfaces to protect our private information. We designed the religions that pitted us against one another. We designed social networks without any way of dealing with abuse or harassment. We designed a financial incentives system that would lead Mark Zuckerberg to assert what's good for the world isn't necessarily good for Facebook; and lead Jack Dorsey to believe engagement was a more important metric than safety. Either by action or inaction, through fault or ignorance, we have designed the world to behave exactly as it's behaving right now. These are our chickens coming home to roost.

The world is on its way to ruin and it's happening by design.

Should we survive the current clusterfuck by the very slimmest of margins, this might be a good time to ask ourselves how we got here, what our role was in getting here, and what our role will be in making sure we don't get here again. That's what this book is for.

First of all, writing this book *is* a hopeful act. For this book to matter, we need two things: the desire to do the right thing and enough time to change course. And while we may not be able to do much about the latter, the fact that you picked this up and you're reading it gives me hope for the former.

Let's get some stuff out of the way. The goal of this book isn't to convince you to quit your corporate job and take a gig at a nonprofit. If you work at a nonprofit, great. I love you. Stay there. Help everyone get clean water and free goats. Those things are important, and this book will still be helpful to you.

But if you work in the bowels of a Fortune 500 company, or you work at Facebook or Google, I need you to stay where you are. You're in a position to affect a lot more people than designers who don't work at those places, and the fact that you work at a place like that and are reading a book like this, makes me think you want to do the right thing.

The goal of this book is to help you do the right thing in environments designed to make it easier to do the wrong thing. (If you work at Uber or Twitter, just quit. We'll also be talking about when to walk away later in this book.) We're going to build a toolbox together. We're going to learn how to persuade people. We're going to learn how to design an argument. We're going to learn why building diverse teams is absolutely crucial to doing good work at scale. We're going to learn how to kick the tires on an idea. We're going to learn how to do the job ethically. And we're going to learn how to make the case for better, more sound ideas. Then, if nothing else works, then and only then will we learn how to throw ourselves on the gears of the odious machines we're being asked to create. We're going to learn how being a designer is being a guardian. We're about to become humankind's last line of defense against monsters.

If defending the world from monsters doesn't get you just a little bit excited, this might not be the right book for you.

Design is a big job. It encompasses multitudes. There are as many designers out there as there are things to design. This book is for all of you. I am, by trade, a UX designer. (That phrase may not exist in 10 years.) I design digital things that people interact with. So most of my examples will be from that realm, which is fine because that's where most of the damage is being done. Whether you're an industrial designer, a graphic designer, a fashion designer, a furniture designer, or a designer of Congressional districts—please stick around. I guarantee you'll get something out of this book.

This book is for everyone who designs things, whether they claim the title or not. If you're affecting how a product works in any way whatsoever— you're designing. For example, a product manager who allocates half the resources your team requested to finish a project is most definitely having an impact on the final design. They're designing. They should read this book.

I intend to show you that design is a political act. What we choose to design and more importantly, what we choose *not* to design and, even *more* importantly, who we exclude from the design process—these are all political acts. Knowing this and ignoring it is also a political act, albeit a cowardly one. Understanding the power in our labor and how we choose to use it defines the type of people we are. As the great Victor Papanek once said, "You are responsible for what you put into the world. And you are responsible for the effects those things have upon the world."

Speaking of Victor Papanek, this book wouldn't exist if I hadn't read *Design for the Real World* as a young designer. More than any design book I ever read, that one made me feel like I was home. It's angry. And yet it's full of love for humanity. Its anger comes from seeing an industry with so much possibility, and so many resources, fall so woefully short of helping those who needed help most. Of course Victor was writing this in 1984 and he was writing about industrial design. The very first line of the book:

> *There are professions more harmful than industrial design, but only a very few of them.*

I am writing this in 2019. I have no doubt that if Victor were still alive, and I sat him down and told him how magnificently we'd fucked up the internet, Victor would justifiably lose his shit. I owe it to Victor to write a book as angry as his, and what I lack in his academic precision, I will make up with more anger and as much hope and love as I can muster. Because while I may yell at you, I do it because I love this thing we do. I love that when we do it right, we help people *so* much.

Is this going to be an incredibly dry and academic book about ethics filled with trolley problems?

Great question. No, it's not. First off, I couldn't write that book. I went to a state school. My vocabulary is blessedly limited and I've never found a fifty dollar word that couldn't be replaced by a nickel word. All the experience I'm putting into this book comes from the field. I've been earning a living as a designer for over twenty years. In that time, I've been asked to design things that would lie to users, trick subscribers, and hold customers hostage. I didn't enjoy doing those things, but for a time I did them because I thought that was the job, and it didn't occur to me that asking myself whether I was doing the right thing was allowable. Once I finally stood up for myself (and for the people who'd be victimized by the unethical work I was doing), I was offered more money to keep doing it or told that "nobody would need to know I did it." Never do work you're ashamed of putting your name on. This book is penance for the work I did early in my career.

Secondly, you wouldn't read a dry academic book about ethics. Not to piss you off, but that book's been written a thousand times—and you didn't read it. There's a reason everybody hates moral philosophy professors: they write incredibly boring books! This book will talk about practical ethics and ways you can make decisions that help you sleep at night. Because we have too much work to do for you to be reading 800 page moral philosophy books, I'm keeping it short. If you want trolley problems, go watch *Mister Rogers' Neighborhood*. I mean that seriously. Half the lessons in this book were first taught to me by Fred Rogers.

The more pedantic among you will probably make the case that I conflate ethics and morals throughout the book. I'm sure I do. The honest truth is that I just don't care. At no point will I claim to be an ethicist. I'm a designer. My goal is to teach you how to work the right way, and it takes both morals *and* ethics. Understanding the difference between the two is like understanding the difference between a font and a typeface. It's interesting to know, but it's not gonna help you set good type. For the sake of putting it to bed, I'll offer this explanation: Someone who won't bake a wedding cake for a gay couple is making a moral decision. (They're also an asshole, which is a great example of me making a moral judgment.) Someone who'd take the order—and put poison in the cake—is making an unethical decision. Get it?

Why should we trust you?

That's an even better question. The short answer is—you shouldn't. You should trust yourself. My guess (my *hope*) is that there are people in the design field who want to do the right thing, but don't have the tools, can't make the arguments, and don't have the support to have those fights. I'm not blaming you. Even those of you who got the best design education possible probably made it through those programs without an ethics class of some sort. I did. If you're willing to do *anything* for a buck, I doubt this book will change your mind. Then again, I doubt that type of person would still be reading. (By the way, if you don't think you need this book but someone gave it to you as a gift, it's because you're wrong about not needing it, and you have a better friend than you deserve.) But if you're the kind of worker who gets a pang in their stomach about the job you're being asked to do, but are not really sure of how to have that conversation, read on. This book is an attempt to help you realize that you already know what the right thing is! This book may help you frame the arguments you've been wanting to make your whole career.

Once you raise your voice, you will be *amazed* how loud it is.

Is this a book about designers changing the world?

Yes. And no. Let me explain. Because I love you, I need to tell you something: you're not special. You have no unique properties. There is absolutely nothing about you that makes you different than anyone else. Even if you are the most creative person you know, I guarantee there are ten million other people. Just. Like. You.

This is good news.

We're no different than anyone else. We're not special. We're ordinary and we live by the same social contract. Yes, designers can change the world—but it's because we have the same responsibility as every other ordinary person on this planet. And just like everybody else, you need to opt in. We can't afford you not trying. If we're going to get past the current mess, we need everyone to do their part. We need to demand better from ourselves, those we work with, and those we work for. No matter where you work, how big or small your role is, or how much influence you believe you have. (I guarantee it's more than you currently think.)

So the real question isn't whether we can change the world, but how?

The world isn't usually changed by special people. It's changed by ordinary people who take it upon themselves to take a stand because they're trying to lead ordinary lives and something stupid gets in their way. In the words of the great Margaret Mead:

Never doubt that a small group of thoughtful, committed citizens can change the world; indeed, it's the only thing that ever has.

The world is changed by seamstresses like Rosa Parks who refuse to live life as a second-class citizen. The world is changed by electricians like Lech Wałęsa trying to earn a fair wage. The world is changed by girls like Malala Yousafzai who desperately want to go to school. The world is changed by punk activists like Nadya Tolokonnikova, who remind us that "words can break cement." The world is changed by regular kids like David Hogg and Emma Gonzalez, who watched their friends die because previous generations refused to do anything about the gun epidemic. The world is changed by cocky kids like Muhammad Ali, who just want to get their stolen bicycle back. The world is changed by civil servants like Georgia gubernatorial candidate Stacey Abrams, who refused to be defeated by a political system designed to defeat her.

For years, the libertarian con artists of Silicon Valley have been telling us they want to change the world. But when the people at the top tell you they want to change the world, it's generally because they've figured out how to profit even more from those below them. (To be fair, not even in my *wildest dreams* did I think even those dirtbags would be okay normalizing fascism to make that happen. Yet here we are.)

I am telling you, we can change the world because there are more of us regular people than there are of them. More importantly, they cannot design the things they imagine without regular people like us. Our labor is what makes us special, and what gives us power. When we turn that labor into a force for making the world better for the largest number of people possible instead of using it to make a few people even richer than they already are? Then, and only then, we may be actually able to change the world. Then we get to go home and live ordinary lives. I am looking forward to it.

Will it be easy? No. But it might just be worth it.

The Ethics
of Design

Do no harm.

The Hippocratic oath is one of the oldest known ethical codes in the world, traced back to somewhere in the third century BCE. It was written by Hippocrates, the father of western medicine, who was probably beginning to see doctors doing some weird shit. To be fair, he was probably doing weird shit too, but their shit was just a little weirder. So, he sat down and wrote an oath that all doctors needed to swear to before they started their doctoring. Because he was a persuasive dude, they agreed to swear by it. To this day, doctors take the Hippocratic oath before being issued licenses. Designers have neither a code, nor a license to practice. (Yet. We're addressing that later.)

Most professions worth their while, and capable of inflicting harm, have ethical codes of some sort. It's a sign of maturity and responsibility, and there's a price paid for not following it, which may include losing your license to practice. (See how they're tied together?) Doctors, lawyers, journalists, Omar from *The Wire*, even our design cousins the architects all have ethical codes they agree to follow.

Imagine walking into a doctor's office and demanding oxycodone. No good doctor is going to prescribe that kind of drug without a good reason. (Picture the unsavory ones that *would*!) Besides common decency, there are two things preventing your doctor from prescribing oxycodone on demand: it goes against their code of ethics (giving a healthy person a drug they don't need is doing harm), and they'd lose their license if someone finds out. Just as importantly, they've been *trained* to not do that! They know it's bad for you, they know it's ethically wrong, and they know they'll be punished for doing it.

Now imagine your boss running up to your desk and demanding you implement some shitty deceptive pattern to trick your users into doing something they don't want to do. How many of you would do it? How many of you know that's a bad thing to do? How many of you know it's an unethical demand? Also, how many of your bosses know they're making an unethical demand? (I guarantee you the addict trying to get oxycodone from the doctor knows what they're doing is sketchy, making them more honest than your boss.)

How many of you think the two situations aren't comparable because the money is flowing in reverse? For those that do—wrong. They're exactly the same. In each situation, someone is demanding that a person who provides a professional service use their skills unethically. If you believe you need to do what your boss wants because they're paying you, you also need to believe the doctor should provide the oxycodone if the addict is willing to pay for it. The exchange of cash for services doesn't supersede ethics. Following unethical orders won't keep you out of jail.

The internet is a harassment and abuse factory in part because designers implemented things they shouldn't—like Facebook's ad network that allows advertisers to target by race, and because companies didn't implement things they should have—like Twitter's failure to deal with abuse. Whether those designers knew they were behaving unethically is something we may never be able to prove, but we need to at least put a stake in the ground. We can at least take ignorance away as an excuse. We need a code and we need to follow it.

Look, writing this book is placing a bet on hope. There will always be shit-ass designers out there who won't give a damn about behaving ethically, just as there'll always be doctors willing to prescribe you that oxy. I am hoping beyond hope, there are designers out there who *want* desperately to design the right thing and just need a code to follow, a toolkit to use, and professional backup. I am hoping there are more of those than the former. I hope that you are among them.

When I became a designer, I didn't have to take an oath, pass the bar like a lawyer, or get a license to practice. Chances are, neither did you. All we had to do was convince someone to exchange their money for our design skills and—voila!—we were professional designers. Of course, when I became a designer we were mostly making websites to advertise movies, sell pet food online, and to find other websites. That's no longer the case. As I write this in 2019, the tech industry is having its moment of panic. Deservedly so.

We've been designing giant world-wide networks that manage personal relationships, generate abuse and harassment, and can't tell (or don't care about) the difference between a good or a bad actor. We're happy to have Nazis on our platforms because they count as engagement. We're happy to let people post the addresses of parents of slain children because we can sell ads against it. We're also designing "smart" devices that can listen to and watch everything we do in our homes. These things are being designed by people who have no idea what their professional ethical code is, or any recourse to deal with designers who break it. The work we do has become astonishingly complex in the last twenty years. I don't just mean technically complex, that was the easy part. I mean ethically complex. Our field has matured and we need to mature along with it.

Fun fact: "Do no harm", which is the part everyone can quote about the Hippocratic Oath, wasn't in the original text. It got added much later. Codes are living documents. They evolve. It's time for us to evolve too.

And yet, if you mention ethical codes to designers they lose their shit. Mention licensing and they go full *Lord of the Flies*. "We'll never agree on one. Who's going to implement it?" I was once called a fascist for suggesting that designers should have a code of ethics. It should freak you out that gangsters can agree on a code of behavior but designers can't. Crime is more organized than design.

About a year ago, I decided to write a code of ethics. It's open-sourced. Take it. Make it better. Treat it like a living document:

A designer is first and foremost a human being.

Before you are a designer, you are a human being. Like every other human being on the planet, you are part of the social contract. By choosing to be a designer you are choosing to impact the people who come in contact with your work, you can either help or hurt them with your actions. The effect of what you put into the fabric of society should always be a key consideration in your work.

Every human being on this planet is obligated to do their best to leave this planet in better shape than we found it. Everyone on the planet is obligated to respect every other human being on this planet. Designers don't get to opt out.

When you do work that depends on a need for income disparity or class distinctions to succeed, you are failing at your job as a human being, and therefore as a designer.

A designer is responsible for the work they put into the world.

Design is a discipline of action. We make things! They go out into the world and they affect people. People don't look at our interfaces to appreciate them, they use them to get things done in their lives. The things we make have consequences. You are responsible for what you put into the world. The work you produce has your name on it. While it is certainly impossible to predict how any of your work may be used, it shouldn't be a surprise when work that is meant to hurt someone fulfills its mission. We cannot be surprised when a gun we designed kills someone. We cannot be surprised when a database we designed to catalog immigrants gets those immigrants deported. When we knowingly produce work that is intended to harm, we are abdicating our responsibility. When we ignorantly produce work that harms others because we didn't consider the full ramifications of that work, we are doubly guilty.

The work you bring into the world is your legacy. It will outlive you. It will speak for you. What do you want it to say?

A designer values impact over form.

We need to fear the consequences of our work more than we love the cleverness of our ideas.

Design does not exist in a vacuum. Society is the biggest system we can impact and everything you do, good and bad, is a part of that system. Ultimately we have to judge the value of our work based on that impact, rather than any aesthetic considerations. An object that is designed to harm people cannot be said to be well-designed, no matter how aesthetically pleasing it might be, because to design it well is to design it to harm others.

Nothing a totalitarian regime designs is well-designed because it has been designed by a totalitarian regime.

A broken gun is better designed than a working gun. There is no ethical way to design a wall that keeps refugees from safety. A database that keeps tracks of immigrants for the sake of deportation will always be broken.

A designer owes the people who hire them not just their labor, but their counsel.

When you are hired to design something, it is for your expertise. Your job is not just to produce that work but to evaluate the impact of that work. Your job is to relay the impact of that work to your client or employer. Should that impact be negative, it is your job to relay that to your client along with a way, if possible, to eliminate the negative impact of the work. If it's impossible to eliminate the negative impact of the work, it's your job to stop it from seeing the light of day. In other words, we're not hired to just dig a ditch, but to evaluate the economic, sociological, and ecological impact of that ditch. If the ditch fails those tests, it's our job to destroy the shovels.

A designer uses their expertise in the service of others without being a servant. Saying no is a design skill. Asking why is a design skill. Rolling your eyes and staying quiet is not. Asking ourselves *why* we are making something is an infinitely better question than asking ourselves whether we *can* make it.

A designer welcomes criticism.

No code of ethics should protect your work from criticism, be it from clients, the public, or other designers. Instead, you should encourage criticism in order to create better work in the future. If your work is so fragile that it can't withstand criticism, it shouldn't exist. The time to kick the tires on what you've designed comes before those tires hit the road.

The role of criticism, when given appropriately, is to evaluate and improve work. Criticism is a gift. It makes good work better. It keeps bad work from seeing the light of day.

You can't fix a cake once it's been baked. This is why criticism should be asked for and welcomed at every step of the design process. It is how you can increase the chance of your project being successful; get feedback early and often. It is your responsibility to ask for criticism.

A designer strives to know their audience.

Design is the intentional solution to a problem within a set of constraints. To know whether you are properly solving those problems you need to meet the people who are having them. If you are part of a team, your team should strive to reflect those people—even better your team should *include* those people. The more a team includes the audience it is problem-solving for, the more thoroughly it can solve those problems. That team can come at a problem from different points-of-view, from different backgrounds, from different sets of needs and experiences. A team with a single point of view will never understand the constraints they need to design for as well as a team with multiple points of view.

What about empathy? Empathy is a pretty word for exclusion. I've seen all-male all-white teams taking "empathy workshops" to see how women think. If you want to know how women would use something you're designing, get a woman on your design team. They're not extinct. We don't need to study them. We can hire them!

A designer does not believe in edge cases.

When you decide who you're designing for, you're making an implicit statement about who you're not designing for. For years we referred to people who weren't crucial to our products' success as "edge cases." We were marginalizing people. We were making a decision that there were people in the world whose problems weren't worth solving.

Facebook now claims to have two billion users, one percent of two billion people, which most products would consider an edge case, is twenty million people. Those are the people at the margins.

These are the trans people who get caught on the edges of "real names" projects. These are the single moms who get caught on the edges of "both parents must sign" permission slips. These are the elderly immigrants who show up to vote and can't get ballots in their native tongues.

They are not edge cases. They are human beings, and we owe them our best work.

A designer is part of a professional community.

You are part of a professional community, and the way you do your job and handle yourself professionally affects everyone in that community. Just as a rising tide affects all boats, taking a shit in the pool affects all swimmers. If you are dishonest with a client or employer, the designer behind you will pay the price. If you work for free, the designer behind you will be expected to do the same. If you do not hold your ground on doing bad work, the designer behind you will have to work twice as hard to make up for that choice. If a designer leaves a job because they were being asked to behave against their ethical code, and you take that job, you're doing all of us a disservice.

While a designer has a personal obligation to earn a living to the best of their abilities and opportunities, doing it at the expense of other designers is a shit way to make a living. Never throw another designer under the bus to advance your own agenda. This includes public redesigns of someone else's work, spec work, unsolicited work, and plagiarism.

A designer seeks to build their professional community, not divide it.

A designer welcomes a diverse and competitive field.

Throughout their entire career, a designer seeks to learn. That means confronting what they do not know. It means listening to other people's experiences. It means welcoming and encouraging people who come from diverse backgrounds, diverse cultures. It means making space at the table for people whom society has historically kept down. We must make space for marginalized voices to be heard in the profession. Diversity leads to better outcomes and solutions. Diversity leads to better design.

A designer keeps their ego in check, knows when to shut up and listen, is aware of their own biases and welcomes having them checked, and fights to make room for those who have been silenced.

Not hiring someone because they're not a good cultural fit is either elitist, racist, or sexist, or all three.

A designer takes time for self-reflection.

No one wakes up one day designing to throw their ethics out the window. It happens slowly, one slippery slope at a time. It's a series of small decisions that might even seem fine at the time, and before you know it you're designing a filtering UI for the Walmart online gun shop.

Take the time for self-reflection every few months, or after every project. Evaluate the decisions you've made recently. Are you staying true to who you are? Or are you slowly moving your ethical goal posts a few yards at a time with each raise or stock option award?

Have you veered off course? Correct it. Is your workplace an unethical hellmouth? Get another one.

Your job is a choice. Please do it right.

So, there it is. Our first stab at a designer's code of ethics. Like I said above, having a code doesn't preclude us from having bad actors in the field. There will always be a doctor willing to prescribe oxycodone. There will always be designers willing to trick and manipulate people for a paycheck. (I hear Twitter is hiring!) But having a code, and better yet discussing and *agreeing* to a code, is the first step to working responsibly. And recognizing our power. We are not hired hands, we are not pixelpushers, we are not order-takers. We are the defense against monsters.

This code of ethics is far from perfect, but it's a good step forward. It'll need to be updated, improved, argued about, and revised. Which you can do, by the way, on Github. Where people have already started translating it. Like I said, it's open-sourced. So have at it.

Meanwhile, what are all these terrible things that you keep mentioning, Mike?

Great question, let's find out...

PART ONE

How Designers Destroyed the World

"Beloveds, these are some bad, ugly, angry times. And I am so freaked out. Hatred has stolen the conversation. The poor are now voting against themselves. But politics is not about left or right. It's about up and down. The few screwing the many."

"We are paid a ton. Looking forward to my yearly bonus of $100k. Fuck ethics. Money is everything."

Moving Fast and Breaking Things

On March 15, 2019, a white supremacist opened fire on two mosques in Christchurch, New Zealand during evening prayer service.

He murdered fifty people. He was wearing a camera and live-streaming his act of terror. The video went viral across multiple platforms, despite a public outcry to take it down. The platforms were doing exactly what they were designed to do: spread, sensationalize, and drive engagement. As teams across the major platforms attempted to eradicate the video from their services they found out how difficult it is to get a system to stop doing what it's been designed to do. Facebook alone had to remove it 1.5 million times in the first 24 hours. This shouldn't have been a shock. After all, they were the ones who designed it that way.[1]

On April 8, 2018, Buzzfeed reported that popular gay dating app Grindr, with 3.6 million daily active users as of that date, was sharing users' HIV status with two other companies. Their status was included in a larger data dump simply because no one thought *not* to include it. It was designed that way.[2]

In 2014, Facebook ran an experiment on over 600,000 human beings using their service. Facebook filled those users' newsfeed with overwhelmingly negative news to see if it had an effect on those users' mental health. Facebook ran a human mental health experiment on its own users without their consent. Obviously anyone with mental health issues had no opportunity to opt out. Neither did anyone else. It was designed that way.[3]

In 2015, a Black software engineer tweeted out that Google Photos AI was categorizing photos of him and his Blackfriends as "gorillas." By 2018, Wired magazine reported Google had fixed the problem by removing the gorilla characterization from the AI database. Not only was it designed that way, but the problem was in the foundation and it couldn't be fixed without a tear-down.[4]

In 2017, Facebook upped the ante and did an emotional study by analysing the usage patterns of 6.4 million Australian youth on their platform, including 1.9 million high school kids as young as 14 to figure out when they were feeling their most worthless, in order to target them with higher-value ads. It was designed that way.[5]

In January 2018, The Guardian reported that fitness tracking app Strava was publishing the jogging routes of soldiers stationed at military bases (which are typically scrubbed off maps for security reasons). Strava encourages their users to share their routes with others. The soldiers tended to run the perimeter of the camps. Effectively mapping the camps for any terrorist organizations with hostile intentions. It was designed to work that way.[6]

On June 18, 2016, Facebook VP Andrew Bosworth circulated this internal memo:

"We connect people. That's why all the work we do in growth is justified. All the questionable contact importing practices... That can be bad if they make it negative. Maybe it costs someone a life by exposing someone to bullies... Maybe someone dies in a terrorist attack coordinated on our tools."

They knew what they were doing, they saw getting someone killed as the price of doing business. It was designed to work that way.[7]

In 2014, Immigration and Customs Enforcement (ICE) awarded Palantir a $41 million contract to build a database for keeping track of immigrants. ICE considers this database absolutely essential in "discovering targets." Among those listed in that now-operational database are over 2,000 infants forcibly separated from their parents and put in cages, as they applied for refugee status in the United States. This database was built by designers who knew why and for whom they were designing it. It was designed to work this way.[8]

In 2016, Facebook exposed the data of 87 million users to Cambridge Analytica, a company working for the Trump campaign. In 2018, Mark Zuckerberg was pulled before Congress for questioning. Democratic congresswoman Anna Eshoo asked him, "Are you willing to change your business model to protect users' privacy?" His reply: "Congresswoman, I don't know what that means." I believe him. It was designed to work this way.[9]

In March 2017, Emily Chang, author of the excellent *Brotopia*, reported a tweet from a troll asking her to "eat his high-quality sperm" and inviting her to a whipping. Twitter replied that the tweet wasn't in violation of any of their anti-harassment rules.[10]

On July 2018, The Guardian wrote about how smart devices have become a new hunting ground for stalkers, jilted lovers, and exes. The exes, usually male, were using devices they'd set up to keep tabs on their former spouses, usually female. We've disrupted domestic violence. It was designed to work that way.[11]

On July 18, 2018, Mark Zuckerberg announced he's okay with holocaust denial viewpoints on Facebook because people sometimes get things wrong, proving his own point. It was designed to work that way.[12]

On February 22, 2019, the Wall Street Journal reported that Flo Health's Period & Ovulation tracker told Facebook when its users were having their periods or expressing an intent to get pregnant. Flo Health's privacy policy specifically said it wasn't doing this. Flo Health claimed the data was depersonalized. The Wall Street Journal tested that and found that one of the things being shared was an advertising identifier that could be matched to a device or profile. It was designed to work that way.[13]

On November 6, 2016, Donald Trump received 2.9 million fewer votes than Hillary Clinton. The Electoral College—originally designed by elite white men to entice agrarian, slave-owning states to join the union—handed the election to the candidate with fewer votes, who also happened to be a white supremacist. It was designed to work that way.

The world isn't broken. It's working *exactly* as it was designed to work. And we're the ones who designed it. Which means we fucked up.

There are two words every designer needs to feel comfortable saying: "no" and "why." These words are the foundation of what we do. They're the foundation of our ethical framework. If we cannot ask "why," we lose the ability to judge whether the work we're doing is ethical. If we cannot say "no," we lose the ability to stand and fight. We lose the ability to help shape the thing we're responsible for.

Every single one of those examples above could've been stopped by enough people asking "why," saying "no," or a combination of both.

WE ARE ~~GATEKEEPERS~~ THE DEFENSE AGAINST MONSTERS

Victor Papanek, who offered us a path toward developing spines in *Design for the Real World*, referred to designers as gatekeepers.[1] He reminded us of our power, our agency, and our responsibility. He reminded us that labor without counsel is not design. We have a skill-set that people need in order to get things made, and that skill-set includes an inquiring mind and a strong spine. We need to be more than a pair of hands. And we certainly can't become the hands of unethical men.

---

1 When *Design for the Real World* was published in 1971, "gatekeeper" was used as a positive. Victor's intent was that designers were the people who kept bad shit from happening. Because language is an amazing and evolving thing, gatekeeping is now seen as people in power controlling access to resources from those that need it. We'll be going with the new definition, while using different language to honor Victor's intent throughout the book because we're not idiots.

As Victor said, "The only important thing about design is how it relates to people."

We are the defense against monsters. Nothing should be making it through the gate without our labor and our counsel. We are responsible for the effects of our work once it makes it out into the world. What passes through that gate carries our seal of approval. It carries our name. Sure, everyone remembers Frankenstein's monster, but they call it by his maker's name. The worst of what we create will outlive us.

There's no longer room in Silicon Valley to ask why. Companies task designers to move fast and break things. *How* has become more important than *why*. How fast can we make this? How can we grab the most market share? How can we beat our competitors to market? (For those of you thinking that I'm generalizing and that your company is different—I am, and yours may be. I look forward to you going to work every day, turning your company into an ethical utopia, and making a liar out of me.)

The current generation of designers have spent their careers learning how to work faster and faster and faster. While there's certainly something to be said for speed, excessive speed tends to blur one's purpose. Excessive speed gets products through that gate before anyone notices what they are and how foul they smell. When we move fast, we break things. It's one thing to break a database, but when that database holds the keys to intimate relationships and the names of two thousand caged babies, the database isn't the only thing that breaks.

Along with speed, we've had to deal with the amphetamine of scale. Everything needs to be faster and also bigger. It's no longer good enough to be the best in your category. You need to destroy all your competition, burn the sky, and view your competitor as an enemy. That is, until the day you buy them for parts.

When we move fast and break things and those things get bigger and bigger, the rubble falls everywhere, destroying communities and the rising dust blots out the sun.

Again, Facebook claims to have two billion users. (What percentage of those users are Russian bots is currently up for debate.) But as I mentioned earlier, one percent of two billion is twenty million. When you're moving fast and breaking things—this is Facebook's internal motto, by the way—one percent is well within the acceptable margin of error for rolling out new work. Technology companies call these people edge cases, but when your edge case contains twenty million people, you need to be careful about what you're breaking. The cavalier attitude of "moving fast and breaking things" is deadly at that scale.

We need to measure more than profit. We need to slow down and measure what our work is doing out there in the world. We need to measure impact on the people whose lives we're affecting. Then, we need to design things that improve the lives of the people who make them and the people who use them; design things which have a positive impact on society at large.

Twitter saved itself from bankruptcy by allowing fascists to run free and by allowing a seventy-two year-old racist xenophobe to break every single one of its rules because he was bringing them engagement. In 2018, it paid off financially. Twitter finally had its first profitable quarter![14] Jack Dorsey, who is technically an invertebrate, was vindicated. His strategy of turning a blind eye to harassment and abuse while building a giant bullhorn for outrage and white supremacy had paid off. Wall Street was happy. Shareholders were happy. Investors were happy. But children were in cages, immigrants were terrified, and decent people like Heather Heyer[15] were being murdered by the goons Donald Trump was dog-whistling from that platform.

Twitter's profitable quarter came at the expense of democracy, decency, and the safety of the world. Sadly, Jack didn't use his newfound profits to buy himself a spine, but rather a shovel to dig himself in deeper. Shortly after being rewarded for designing a garbage fire, he was once again talking about how *this time* he was serious about cutting down the abuse. It had all the believability of Donald Trump promising to look into election meddling. People don't see the things they're rewarded for as problems to fix.

And as much as I'd like to put that entire disgrace at Jack Dorsey's feet, and heaven knows he deserves it, he simply couldn't have executed that plan without the help of everyone working for him. Every single employee working at Twitter in the last few years saw exactly where it was headed—if they didn't, it's because they weren't looking. While I don't doubt there were a few people trying to right the ship from the inside, you simply cannot correct a problem that management doesn't see as a problem. As Upton Sinclair so eloquently put it:

> It is difficult to get a man to understand something when his salary depends upon his not understanding it.

Twitter never wanted to understand the problem. Their salaries depended on them not understanding the problem. If Twitter believed it had *any* kind of problem, it was a public relations problem.

Twitter employees bore a responsibility to ask "why" and to say "no." When they agreed to work at the company, their job wasn't just to build a tool for the company, but also to understand how the company worked, and to make sure it didn't work in a way that was detrimental to society. This is a burden all designers share, no matter where we choose to work. It's part of the job. For the record, these aren't answers I expect designers to come up with by themselves, but through asking questions and working collaboratively.

In February of 2017, after I'd been badgering him for months, Jack Dorsey agreed to meet me in person. Oddly, he agreed to meet me at Square, his *other* company. (My dad had a bumper sticker on the family Volaré that said *"My* other *car is a Cadillac"* so I totally get it.) We had a civil discussion. He was a gracious host, and I was a gracious guest. I asked him how he justified keeping Donald Trump on Twitter. I asked him how he justified not banning known white supremacists like David Duke and Mike Cernovich. In both cases, he gave me the free speech spiel he has memorized. He also told me there was a plan to deal with it, but they had to get it right. There was going to be a magical algorithm that took care of everything. He didn't say magical. That's my take. Jack was looking for a magical formula to fix everything. All at once. Without having to get his hands dirty. The fascists would get kicked out as soon as Twitter launched the algorithm that magically fixed anything. His approach was as passive as that sentence. Jack's main priority was making sure he couldn't be accused of having made a decision. His obsession with remaining impartial has made him impotent to act, even on the side of decency. He wants to be able to cast blame on an algorithm, rather than his own actions. That way he wouldn't have any blood on his hands.

Except the blood is already there. It's all over the people who've been silenced. How is it free speech when it silences so many? I'm all for protecting free speech. Let's start by amplifying the voices of those who've been silenced, not protecting the voices of those who've silenced them. A system that protects bullies isn't a system we should be putting our labor into.

An algorithm is not a spine.

The boy kings of Silicon Valley love a good algorithm—they've designed some great ones over the years. But there are problems even the best math can't solve. There are times when you physically have to walk over to a server and pull the plug. I get why they want an algorithm to do it—lack of accountability. Intentionally pulling the plug on someone who's trolling women on your service is a decision. It requires agency, leadership, and a point of view. But should that troll get caught in an algorithm? Well, that's a different matter. There was no intent to *specifically* get rid of that person. A good algorithm is the equivalent of breaking up with someone over a text message and then turning your phone off. It's cowardly. Good leaders should aspire to have their fingerprints all over hard decisions.

By the way, I offered to walk over and turn off Trump's account myself. Jack didn't take me up on it.

My dad has a small garden out back. In his old age, he's decided to grow things. Tomatoes, zucchini, cabbage, the assortment of herbs... standard stuff. A few years ago, he called me all pissed off because foxes have attacked his garden.

"What are you gonna do?"

"Put up a fence."

That's exactly what he did. He put up a fence. The foxes figured out how to get under the fence. He then dug a moat and filled it with concrete. The foxes found another way in. His neighbors, who are used to my Dad going to war with the local wildlife, suggested poison.

"I don't want to kill them. I just don't want them in my damn garden!"

My dad understood that if he ever wanted a tomato out of that garden he had to fight tooth and nail every day. He had to be vigilant. He had to adapt. He fought foxes. He fought weeds. There were probably a few groundhogs mixed in there. But he understood that garden required tending to grow. Most importantly, he understood he was responsible for bringing the seeds he planted to fruit. He never did manage to keep the foxes out completely, but he stayed vigilant enough that he remained a step ahead of them.

Last time I was at my folks' house, my dad made a salad. Told me everything in it came from his garden.

"These tomatoes are delicious dad."

"Best fucking tomatoes *you* ever ate."

They were indeed.

WHO DO DESIGNERS WORK FOR?

I've been working in client services for almost twenty years. That's long enough to learn a few things. One of the things I learned along the way was that clients (this goes for bosses as well) need to know who they are hiring and what it's going to be like to work together before they actually agree to work together. Because I've had one too many arguments with clients that ended with, "I sign your paychecks and you will do what I say," I composed a little thing we tell our clients before they agree to work with us:

"You may be hiring us and that may be your name on the check, but we do not work for you. We're coming in to solve a problem, because we believe it needs to be solved and it's worth solving. But we work for the people being affected by that problem. Our job is to look out for them because they're not in the room. And we will under no circumstances design anything that puts those people at risk."

Ballsy, eh? Only a few potential clients refused to move forward after hearing that. Trust me, I'd say it in a nice way. I'm a people person. Anyone who refused to work with us after hearing that was doing us a favor. They were probably going to be a nightmare client. More often than you'd expect, the reply we got was, "Awesome. That's exactly what I want."

Here's the important thing: I absolutely believe every word of what I said. When you hire me as a designer, I do not work for you. I may practice my craft at your service, but you haven't earned the right to shape how I practice that craft. One, you don't want me designing at your level, you want me designing at mine. That means you don't get to pull the strings, I do. Two, you're hiring someone who performs a service, not a servant. There's a difference. I'm not there to do your bidding, I'm there to solve a problem or reach a goal that we agreed upon.

So, who do designers work for?

Throughout this book, I'm gonna pull a little trick where I look at other professions to examine how those professionals behave in certain situations and then attempt to map that behavior over to what designers do. This is helpful because it gives us a bit of distance and allows us to learn from people who've already solved similar problems. Or, as my mom would say when she took me and my brothers out to dinner and we behaved like assholes, "You see that table over there? You see how they're not throwing food at each other? The parents won't be divorced in a year. And the kids will grow up to be doctors." This may be why I write about doctors so much, by the way.

Like I mentioned in the previous chapter, doctors take an oath before they begin practicing. This doesn't ensure they're all going to behave ethically, but if they're going to behave badly, they certainly can't claim ignorance. Now, once they take that oath, they can go off and do a variety of things. Some enter private practice. Some join organizations like Médecins Sans Frontières. Some go to work in top-of-the-line hospitals, serving patients with lots of insurance. Some go to work at free clinics. A lot of them end up doing a combination of those things. But no matter where they go, the oath they took determines how they behave on the job. They'll certainly face constraints along the way, such as a lack of the latest equipment at the hospital where they're working. But their job is to do their job, as defined by their code, to the best of their abilities.

Pay attention, because this is where the comparison goes into high gear. Now imagine a doctor runs into a sketchy hospital administrator who's trying to keep a hospital afloat by telling doctors to order tests patients don't need, or to prescribe medications from pharmaceutical companies the administrator's made deals with, or charging people for services they didn't receive. You get the idea. This isn't much different than working for a boss who asks you to target poor people with addictive products, or to collect user data you don't need in case the company might want to sell it later. Except when a doctor is asked to do those things, the oath they took supersedes the signature on their paycheck and they understand that by committing those acts they're violating their oath. When a designer faces these issues, there's no oath in place. We have no official ethical framework to fall back on. You may get a gut feeling that what you're doing is wrong and it may not feel good to do it, but at no point in your career have you actually put pen to paper or hand over heart and promised not to behave this way.

More importantly, if a doctor is caught behaving unethically, there's a fairly good chance they could lose their license. A designer who behaves unethically for a shady boss might get a raise. Your shady boss now knows they have someone they can rely on for shady work.

But people die when doctors do their jobs badly, Mike! Yeah, well...

In 2017, the Royal Society of Public Health in the UK, in conjunction with the Young Health Movement published a study about how social media affects young people's mental health.[16] It's worth reading in its entirety, but let me highlight the part salient to what we're discussing. Between 2010 and 2015, after a twenty-year decline, teenage suicide started rising again, along with rates of anxiety, depression, body dysmorphia, etc.

"Social media has been described as more addictive than cigarettes and alcohol, and is now so entrenched in the lives of young people that it is no longer possible to ignore it when talking about young people's mental health issues."

—Shirley Cramer, chief executive, Royal Society for Public Health

While the study doesn't make a conclusive connection between mental health and social media because of academic rigor and all that, it makes a very strong case for it. Thankfully, I'm not an academic, and I have little patience for academic pussyfooting, as well-meaning as it may be. So I have no problem telling you this: the work we are doing is *killing people*. A Google search for "deaths by social media" will bring up more examples than you should need.

Those of us who grew up designing things online need to realize the repercussions of the work we do. We're no longer pushing pixels around a screen. We're building complex systems that touch people's lives, destroy their personal relationships, broadcast words of both support *and* hate, and undeniably mess with their mental health. When we do our jobs well, we improve people's lives. When we don't, people die.

So, yes. The comparisons to the medical profession are apt.

OUR INEFFICIENCIES ARE OUTSTANDING

I was taking the tram home one evening, and realized I'd left my headphones at the office—meaning I had to listen to people on the train coming home from their startup jobs. I heard two tech dudes arguing about how to set up a server. I heard two other dudes arguing about data collection; and I watched the dude next to me do some coding. On a fifteen-inch laptop. On a crowded train car.

When we got to my stop, the doors wouldn't open because of some technical malfunction. Everyone waited (mostly) patiently as the driver got out and opened each door one by one—which wasn't quick. While he did that, the two tech dudes talking about setting up a server changed topics to how bad San Francisco's public transportation can be. (They're not wrong.) One mentioned how inefficient the city was. He pointed out the tram stops are all different. Sometimes underground, sometimes above ground. Sometimes there's a platform. Sometimes the steps have to be lowered to meet the street. Sometimes the doors open on the left; sometimes on the right. The other guy replied that things would certainly run a lot smoother and more efficiently if we standardized all of that.

He's not wrong.

Society runs more efficiently when all the metro stops are the same, and all the streets are a certain width. And everyone just agrees to behave the same way, follow the same rules, and eat the same thing. (Soylent is *very* efficient.) We could all wear the same shoes. (Allbirds are *very* comfortable.) What if we all voted the same? And spoke the same language?

When I was a little baby designer, I was taught that good design meant simplifying. Keep it clean. Keep it simple. Make the system efficient, with as few variations as possible. I'm sure the same goes for setting up style sheets, servers, and all that other shit we do. My city *would* run more efficiently if we simplified everything.

But I wouldn't want to live there.

My city is a fucking mess. My country is a fucking mess. The internet is a fucking mess. But in none of those cases is the whole answer to look for efficiencies. We need to celebrate the differences. Celebrate the reasons the metro stops aren't all the same. Celebrate the crooked streets. Celebrate the different voices. Celebrate the different food smells. Understand that other people like things you don't, and you might like things *they* don't. And it's all cool! That's what makes this city, and all cities, a blast. When all these amazing people, some of whom we don't understand at all, go online, they are going to behave as inefficiently in there as they do out there. That is awesome.

Your job, the glorious job you signed up for when you said you wanted to be a designer, is to support all of these people. To make sure none of these incredible voices get lost. And to fight against those who see that brilliant cacophony as a bug and not the greatest feature of all time.

You are our protection against monsters.

Society doesn't serve Silicon Valley. Silicon Valley needs to serve society. We are big. We are multiple. And we are amazingly inefficient. And of course, we don't all want the same thing, do we? Except that yes, we *actually* do.

We all want to thrive.

Ayn Rand Was a Dick

Let's talk about ride-sharing.

At an abstract level, ride-sharing is the idea that people who have cars and a little extra time can provide a service to people who need rides and are willing to pay for them. At an abstract level, it takes an underused resource and puts it to use. It benefits both sides of the equation. The driver gets to make a little extra cash, and the passenger gets the ride they need. Sounds okay so far. In fact, ride-sharing even has the potential to reduce the number of cars on the road. Win-win. All you have to do is figure out how to get the two sides to connect.

It turns out that's not so hard. In 2009, Travis Kalanick figured out how to do it. (You can argue about his role in inventing this all you want. I really don't care. It's not important to the story and truth is, he made the most noise at the table, so he's the one who gets the bill.) Travis and his small team of white boys—an important detail, wait for it—developed an app that connected the drivers with the riders. That app was, of course, Uber.

At an abstract level, this was great. Every party involved in the equation did well, including Travis and his team—which is fair. They did the job of connecting everyone. At this point in our story, we have total balance. The drivers are making a little cash; the rider is getting where they need to get for a fair amount; and Uber and the team are skimming a little off the top for making the connection. Theoretically, this story could continue like this for a while, with the incremental improvement here and there, the occasional hurdle to jump (gotta deal with those taxi unions, Travis!), and eventual attempts at slow and steady growth. At some point, conditions in the marketplace would change and Uber would either collapse (think Blockbuster) or adapt (think Netflix).

If that were the beginning and end of the Uber story, I wouldn't be writing about it. Small successes built incrementally over time don't make for dramatic stories or good ethical lessons. So, it's time to introduce a villain. Oh! You thought Travis was the villain? That's fair, but we hadn't fully fleshed him out yet. He's like James Franco at the beginning of Spider-Man. You *know* he's eventually gonna fuck someone over, but he hasn't gotten his motivation yet. He's about to. Let's give this story a location.

Welcome to Silicon Valley. A libertarian stronghold at the very end of America. (Literally.) Silicon Valley, and specifically the venture capital firms of Silicon Valley, are mostly run by old white men who read Ayn Rand in high school, thought it was great, and never changed their minds. (This is where I need to be fair and let you know that not *all* venture capitalists are monsters. In fact, I'm friends with a few who are lovely people. They are very much the exceptions. Also, every VC who reads this book will think this parenthetical is about them.) In the words of the late great Ann Richards, they were "born on third base and think they hit a triple."

For those of you not familiar with Ayn Rand, she wrote crappy books about the power of individual achievement while she collected social security and started some pseudo-philosophy called "objectivism," which can be summed up in five words: I got mine, fuck you. The old white men of Silicon Valley all have giant Ayn Rand back tattoos. (Look, it's a chapter about venture capitalism inside an ethics book. I gotta tell a joke once in a while, for all our benefit.)

Venture capital firms invest in new companies. Like Uber. In fact, it's not unheard of that they'd invest in Uber and also a company that Uber considers a competitor. They're not loyal. They're placing bets. They invest a small amount in exchange for a percentage of the company, and if that company does well, they'll invest more in exchange for another percentage of the company. If the company doesn't do well, well, that's fine. Venture capitalists place a lot of bets, and they don't expect the majority of them to pan out. But when those bets do pan out, the goal becomes what venture capitalists call a liquidity event. The exit involves taking the startup public, or more likely, selling it to a bigger company for a ton more money than initially invested (ten times more being the rule of thumb). The companies that don't make it are sold off for parts.

Again, in the abstract, like ride-sharing, the venture capital model isn't unethical. New companies are risky. New companies need capital. It's how people behave within these models that's messed up.

Let's go back to Uber. Once a company gets funding, its goal changes from building a successful business to reaching a liquidation event. Because once you get funding, your investors are pushing you to grow faster and faster, and to get there you're going to need another round or two or three of funding. Venture capital is like startup cocaine. Once you get a taste, your job changes from connecting drivers and riders to getting another hit.

All of a sudden, your tiny little startup needs to hire 5000 drivers a week, so background checks get a little streamlined. You need to hire 500 engineers a week, and no way those are all top-notch. You need to hire 300 designers a month, so you just start strip-mining design schools and picking up a lot of inexperienced people. You need to expand into more cities, so you skip the delicate political negotiations that it takes to ensure there's an ecological balance there. Keep in mind these decisions are often being made by young people who, while possibly being extremely skilled, have little-to-no management experience. It's at this point the quality that once made you good enough to attract attention in the first place takes a nosedive. Now the company's job isn't to show quality, it's to show growth.

It's at this point that Uber started charging riders higher fares, including notoriously implementing surge pricing during disasters, such as during the 2015 terrorist attack in Paris. They also started skimming more off the top from their drivers, leading up to an infamous incident where a driver asked Travis Kalanick why this was happening, and Travis proceeded to dress down a person attempting to make a living off his service. (The driver was good enough to record it for all of us.[17]) It's also at this point where complaints about drivers being abusive to riders started to rise, for which Uber had an interesting solution: they implemented a harassment campaign against Sarah Lacy, the journalist bringing these stories to the public's attention. (Uber Senior Vice President Emil Michael, told Buzzfeed reporter Ben Smith the company was contemplating doing opposition research into Sarah Lacy's private life.[18] He later apologized.)

Hold on, we're not done. At some point n 2017, Uber designed a tool called Greyball, which they used to flag riders they believed were associated with cities officials or regulatory bodies Uber had labeled as enemies. (NY Times reporter Mike Isaac did an excellent job exposing this. He's currently writing a book about Uber. Read it when it comes out.) Greyball tracked phone numbers associated with those "enemies," who were then told there were no cars available when they used the app. This was fraud. Everyone involved in the conception, design, execution, and maintenance of that tool acted unethically.

Once Uber's goal moved from providing a car-sharing service to using a car-sharing service to make themselves and their investors rich, the delicate balance between drivers, riders, and Uber was destroyed. Only one of those parties was going to benefit from Uber's future success. There's nothing wrong with making money, but there is something inherently wrong with profiting from the labor of others without giving them a piece of the success they've earned.

Uber set out to build a tool that democratized access to cars. It ended up building a tool that further impoverished the poor. The service model was fine, but the financial model it used for growth could only ever be as ethical as the people who strove to benefit the most.

Sadly, Uber is not an exception, but the rule and aspiration in Silicon Valley. Take a bunch of entitled white boys, give them a ton of money, fill them with the fear of the money running out, and you've created a perfect recipe for inexperienced people making really bad short-term decisions that have a tendency to fuck everything up. (To be fair, in Travis' defense, he did have the experience. He's just a dick.)

Short-term decisions are all Silicon Valley seems to care about. We don't build businesses for the long haul anymore, at least not the venture-backed ones. Those only need to last long enough to make it to their liquidity event so the investors can get their payday. So, if Uber can show growth by squeezing drivers and riders, and Twitter can increase their engagement numbers by relying on white supremacists and outrage, and Facebook can rake in some extra cash from Russian fake news sites—they will do it. And we know they'll do it, because they did it. Silicon Valley has exhibited total comfort with destroying the social fabric of humanity to make a profit.

I got mine. Fuck you.

LET'S TALK ABOUT IGNORANCE, BUT NOT THE BAD KIND

In 1971, American philosopher John Rawls proposed an idea for determining the ethics of a situation, he called it a veil of ignorance. He later expanded on the idea in his book *A Theory of Justice*. In short, a veil of ignorance is a way of determining whether what you're designing, be it a startup, a dinner plan, or a system of government, is just. It's very simple: when designing something, imagine that your relationship to that system gets determined *after* you've made it. For example, if you're designing a system of government that allows slavery, you might end up being enslaved. If you're designing a ride-sharing service, you might end up as the driver or the rider.

With a veil of ignorance in place, you see yourself from the rider's perspective and you might start considering things like what to do if the driver makes a pass at you. Of course, this is more likely to be considered when your team includes women. You ask yourself how to handle situations where the driver refuses to pick you up. Of course, your team is more likely to consider situations like that when it includes Black men, who notoriously have a hard time getting a cab to stop for them.[19] You can also put yourself in the driver's position and ask yourself how you'd handle a rowdy drunk in your cab. Or what you'd do if you realized everyone on the app side of the ride-sharing ecosystem was racking up options and higher salaries while your cut kept decreasing.

Designing with a veil of ignorance in place increases the odds that what we're designing is just, and it also increases the chances that we're not destroying the ecosystem that benefits us. The drivers, the riders, and the creators of the app that brought them together all need each other to survive. They should all share the benefits of success equally.

Like I said at the beginning of this chapter, the system itself wasn't unethical by nature, but the actors within it were. Any system eventually bends to the ethics of those designing it, but also to those investing in it, because they have as much of a hand in designing a product as anyone, sometimes more. When the credo of the people making the tool is "I got mine, fuck you," the system reflects that.

There is no such thing as neutral software. We all bring our own biases to the things we design—our own ethical code, and our own garbage.

Ultimately, what we're designing isn't an assortment of individual apps and services, it's an ecosystem. As long as Silicon Valley is putting money into services that profit from making one class of people (themselves) richer, while making everyone else around them poorer, while demanding tax subsidies from the cities where they build their self-contained castles (Remember Ayn Rand living off social security?), we are fucked. As long as designers work within this system, we are complicit.

SO WHERE DOES THIS LEAVE US?

Take a deep breath because before I can start making you feel better, I need you to feel worse. I am writing this book in 2019 in San Francisco, California. I am writing from the end of America, possibly in more ways than one. I'm an immigrant in this country and our government is putting refugee children in cages and beginning to discuss denaturalizing citizens. Before you throw this book across the room and scream that you didn't buy a design book to read about politics, one—I warned you that I would, and two—we need to talk about it. Because this is the story of where we put our labor, and where we put our labor is a choice; a choice that we should be willing and able to make with our eyes wide open, fully aware of its repercussions. Who we work for and how we do that work are the only things that matter right now.

The real question isn't how you're going to pay your rent or mortgage while working ethically, the *real* question is why you'd be willing to work unethically in the first place.

As designers, we have an ethical responsibility to the entire ecosystem that we design within. Our job isn't just to make money for ourselves, although we can't ignore that. Our job isn't just to make money for those who hire us, although we can't ignore that either. Our job isn't just to do work that delights the people who use it, although we can't ignore that. Ultimately, our job is to do *all* of those things in equal measure and also in a way that benefits the society that supports us all.

When we find ourselves working in a system that favors one side of the equation over others, it's our job to correct the system. You want a design problem? There it is. The biggest design problem of our time. How do we work in Silicon Valley within a system that favors profit for one side of the equation over the livelihood of all others? How do we work within a system run by people who believe "getting theirs" justifies every decision they make, because they cling to a puerile mentality of an ideology that hyenas, the Libertarians of the animal world, would discard as too spoiled?

One answer is, obviously, that we don't. We walk away. We go off and design stuff with nonprofits and NGOs and other people who do good works. Or we walk away from the craft forever, buy a goat farm or spend our days helping youth-in-crisis. For some of us, that might be the right answer. (I can't guarantee that in time I won't go this route myself.) There's absolutely no shame in deciding this isn't the life for us or that we've reached the end of our fight. If you're ready to hang 'em up, go in peace and thank you for your service. Or if you walked into this craft believing that it would be all personal vision, bliss, and mood boards for your favorite brands, this might be your exit.

Another possible answer is the old percentage trick. In fact, Victor Papanek (his name's gonna come up a lot; just get used to it) was a believer in designers donating ten percent of their time to nonprofit causes or good works, as a way to make up for what they did the other ninety percent of the time. On this, and maybe only this, Victor and I disagree. There's no percentage of your time that can make up for building databases that round up immigrants for ICE while you work at Palantir. There's no percentage of your time that can make up for building facial ID software (also for ICE) while working at Microsoft. (In fact, those employees rebelled and forced Microsoft to cancel that contract.) There's no percentage of your time that can make up for allowing white supremacists to run free on Twitter. I don't believe in ethical offsets. There's no way that saving ten percent of the world while destroying ninety percent of it turns into anything close to a net positive.

The last possible way that we can answer this question is the hardest. We work within the system by doing our jobs. By doing our jobs the way we define them to be, the way we need them to be, the way society needs us to do them. If you're thinking, "Oh shit, this fool thinks we're Jedi or something!" well, you're not far off.

Look, it's really easy to tell you not to work in organizations that do unethical shit, like weapons manufacturing, the private prison industry, or the Catholic Church. That stuff's easy to avoid and it's fairly self-se-

Ayn Rand filling out Social Security paperwork.

lecting. But remember how I started this chapter talking about how in the abstract, there was nothing wrong with Uber? That's still true. That's the stuff we need to worry about. If this were as easy as not working for unethical industries, I wouldn't be a writing you a book. I'd be making you a list. Asking ourselves whether something is ethical isn't just a thing to do when deciding to take a job, it's a thing we need to ask ourselves every day we're on that job.

When I look out at today's political landscape at the companies that destroyed democracy and increased income disparity, I see social networks, I see open-source blogging tools, I see the sharing economy. I see services that might very well have passed that first ethical test. I see companies that, for the most part, were created with the best of intentions falling into a system that rewards growth, regardless of how it comes. In fact, Silicon Valley champions the idea of disruptive growth and in their Randian-fueled haze of dime-store objectivism, they see anyone trampled by that growth as not being fit enough to survive. What we need to worry about isn't unethical industries. It's unethical decisions made over time because of ill-conceived motivations.

We built the networks that brought this world to ruin. We built the digital megaphones that brought the alt-right to power, and when we realized what was happening, we refused to do anything about it because of the money it was bringing in. And while the decision on what course to take is made at the top of these organizations, like Jack Dorsey refusing to budge an inch on abuse or harassment, ultimately their decisions cannot be implemented without our labor.

And there, right *there*—there is our power. Labor.

LET'S FIGHT MONSTERS!

You know that line about every group of friends having at least one asshole and if you can't figure out who it is, it's probably you? Right. Well, every place you work has someone responsible for making sure the work you're doing is ethically sound. I'll give you a minute to figure out who it is.

Please tell me you got that.

Working the right way requires constant vigilance. It's why we've learned to ask "why" and to say "no." That vigilance is required of everyone you work with, but you also can't expect that someone else is taking care of it, and working at a place that's not making good ethical choices doesn't absolve you from having to make them yourself. I've travelled around the world talking to designers about ethics and one of the lines I hear repeated over and over is from designers trying to get absolution from working ethically: "If I don't do it, someone else will."

That's lazy logic, and you're smarter than that.

Just because someone else is willing to be a dick shouldn't be enough of an excuse for you to be one. Just because your boss asks you to implement something fraudulent isn't enough of an excuse for you to do it. When no one else around you is asking the hard questions, when no one else around you is standing up for the people who entrust their personal information and their relationship statuses to your service... that's when we need you the most.

Rather than deciding the fight is lost before it's even started, consider that standing up for the right thing might just be the spark that ignites others. I honestly believe there are more people out there who want to do the right thing than people who want to do the wrong thing. Be the one who motivates those around you to behave their best. And if the person next to you should be the one who says, "Hey, this doesn't seem quite right," be the one who backs them up. You're not alone.

Remember the Microsoft workers I mentioned above? In July of 2018, after ICE started separating refugee families at the US/Mexican borders and putting their children in cages, it came to light that Microsoft had subcontracted with ICE on face-recognition software they were using to identify undocumented Americans. While it's true that Microsoft employees built the software in the first place, finding out it was being used by the agency putting children in cages was their line in the sand. They got together and they demanded that leadership cancel the ICE contract. They were successful.

The people doing the work have a tremendous amount of power in these situations. That's you! Are there repercussions? Absolutely. You might lose your job, and in America, that's likely to mean your health insurance as well. (That's by design.) What you need to understand is that there are repercussions either way. When the work we do (and facial recognition software is definitely in our wheelhouse) can be used to put children in cages, we have to ask ourselves whether *those* repercussions are more or less terrible than the repercussions we might face for fighting it. As the employees of Microsoft found out, you can fight and win.

If only the employees at Twitter had the same courage, we could've avoided a lot of this.

Ayn Rand was a dick but we don't have to be. When we are brought in to our work, we need to come in with all the tools. That includes an ethical code that goes beyond and above anything else that you might find waiting for you at your cubicle, in your company's "vision statement," or the cafeteria. A doctor's ethical code doesn't ebb and flow depending on what hospital employs them. The code is the code. It needs to be the same with designers. We need to do our job at an ethical level that goes beyond that of the people for whom we work.

A designer's job is always to look out for society's best interest. Sadly, at this particular moment in time, Silicon Valley's goals run counter to that. This is why we need to stay and fight. We have people counting on us.

We have more power than we think. Trust me on that.

From Bauhaus to Courthouse

In September of 2015, Volkswagen was caught lying about diesel engine emissions.

Since 2008, they had been marketing a wide range of passenger vehicles as high performance, fuel-efficient, and low emissions—low enough to meet the toughest environmental standards in the world, earning green car subsidies and tax benefits. Except these cars weren't that clean. In order to deliver performance and fuel economy—the things drivers notice—they were releasing far more pollution into the air than Volkswagen claimed. So, Volkswagen came up with a solution. They designed and installed software into around 11 million cars to detect and deceive emissions testing.[20] The programming—called a "defeat device"—would direct the engine to activate all the emissions controls for the duration of the test—the equivalent of a child behaving well only while being watched. The cars would pass the test with flying colors, then hit the road emitting ten to forty times more nitrogen oxides than allowed by US regulations.

Volkswagen built a tool that lied to customers, testing stations, the general public, and yes—to shareholders. Thanks to several years of independent research on discrepancies between lab tests and road tests, the EPA found out and opened an investigation. The US Justice Department set out to see whether Volkswagen had defrauded people. The US Justice

Department cares about fraud. (This was pre-Trump. Obviously.) One of the judicial tests for fraud is intent. Intent is notoriously hard to prove, unless the company committing the fraud has put together a detailed Powerpoint presentation illustrating the purpose and function of the software—which Volkswagen had (apparently unaware of Stringer Bell's admonition, "Is you taking notes on a criminal fucking conspiracy? The fuck is you thinking, man?" Your annoying friend is right; everyone needs to watch *The Wire*.)

James Liang was an engineer at Volkswagen. He designed the software that lied about Volkswagen's diesel emissions. During the subsequent trial, a group of experts reverse-engineered James' software and concluded that it couldn't have been designed to do what it did without James being aware.

On August 25, 2017, James Liang was sentenced to forty months in prison for bad design. (Sadly, I'm guessing the reason he ended up in jail has more to do with deceiving shareholders than lying to customers *or* destroying the environment.) James was a middleman. He accepted orders and he fulfilled them, like most of us. James Liang was following the orders of unethical leaders and in doing so, he became unethical himself.

Eventually, all of this ended up costing James Liang forty months of his life, Volkswagen CEO Martin Winterkorn his job (Don't cry for Martin. He got a $10 million golden parachute), and Volkswagen a $14.7 billion court settlement. More importantly, their fraud really messed with our air.

It's also worth noting the forty-month sentence was more prison time than federal prosecutors were seeking. James had cooperated with the prosecution and expressed regret for his actions during the trial. The judge wasn't having it. "Your cooperation and regret is noted, but it doesn't excuse the conduct," he said as he passed sentence.

Cooperation and regret is noted, but it doesn't excuse the conduct. At some point in their lives, the people who helped Mark Zuckerberg, Jack Dorsey, and Travis Kalanick execute their schemes may regret what they've done, they may even cooperate in undoing it. But, like the judge said—it won't excuse the conduct.

Here's the *really* interesting part: we can go to jail for this shit now!

Recently, I went back and reread *The Jungle* by Upton Sinclair. I did it because I'd been using the famous quote—"It is difficult to get a man to understand something, when his salary depends upon his not understanding it"—in conference talks and I thought I should reacquaint myself with the novel. I hadn't read it since high school and I was surprised by how much I'd forgotten. (Not really. I was probably high as a kite the first time around.) *The Jungle* is the story of the meat packing industry at the beginning of the 20th century, an industry which had become so foul and so unethical and so vile, they were willing to package and sell diseased meat to the public. The book sold like uncontaminated hotcakes and became a best seller. Readers freaked out about the working conditions that Sinclair described in the book. They got skittish about eating meat, and eventually, then-President Theodore Roosevelt appointed a commission to see if what Sinclair had described was true. It was. All of this led to the Meat Inspection Act of 1906, which increased government regulations on the meat industry and put them under the watchful eye of the Department of Agriculture.

If any of this is reminding you of Jack Dorsey and Mark Zuckerberg testifying before congress in late 2018, I assure you that it's on purpose.

The tech industry is at the exact same place now as the meat packing industry was when *The Jungle* came out. For years, the startups of Silicon Valley have screamed disruption while the libertarian boy-kings at the helms shoveled maggot-infested, rancid, addictive software at us. They still scream about disruption as they beg cities for tax breaks. They scream about the evils of regulation as they continue to exclude already marginalized people from their ranks. They babble on about freedom of speech while they protect the rights of bullies to silence the vulnerable. They deny their workers benefits and personal lives. They make their quarterly profits by accepting payments in rubles to insert fake foul news into the same timeline as your children's photos.

So the next time you're in the company cafeteria and someone's going on about disruption, as they enjoy their lovingly prepared locally-sourced meat—ask them why they feel safe eating it. Ask them how they're sure their meal is maggot-free or that it hasn't been sitting in a stockyard under a blazing summer sun for a week. Turns out, we're all in favor of regulations when it comes to what we shovel into our mouth. Not so much when we're spewing ideas about disrupting the cities we live in.

Everyone should read *The Jungle*—especially people working in Silicon Valley and tech, because this industry is going through that same moment in its evolution right now. We're moving fast. We're breaking things. And we're up to our necks in shit. We have no idea how, or in some cases have no desire to, fix the rampant abuse and harassment in the tools we make. Especially when our paychecks depend on us not fixing those things. We're following the orders of unethical people. (To be fair, the European Union is doing better on this than the US. Read on.)

The lesson I'm trying to convey with all this is a big one—we can go to jail for this shit now!

James Liang went to prison because the automobile industry is regulated. In fact, it was *during* one of those regulatory tests that we found out Volkswagen was bamboozling the public! Regulations work. There's a reason why Travis Kalanick violently insisted that Uber was a software company and not an automotive company. He didn't want to fall under the automobile industry's regulation. When Uber built Greyball to deceive cities' attempts to regulate Uber within their city limits, what his team did was no different than what James Liang's team did—they purposely and knowingly deceived people who were looking out for public safety. Except Uber wasn't bound by the same types of regulatory bodies. That is going to change. One way or another, we have fucked up this industry too much to continue along this path. The only question at this point is whether we are going to regulate ourselves, by adopting a higher standard of ethics, or whether we want to wait until the government steps in and does it for us.

On May 25, 2018, tens of thousands of businesses had to review, and in most cases revise, how they were collecting user data and what user data they were collecting to comply with the European Union's General Data Protection Regulation (GDPR). The GDPR not only regulates what you can collect, but how soon you need to report a data breach. This applied to *any* organization with business ties to the EU. That's pretty much any online service you use and most likely the company that cuts your checks. The cost of non-compliance is some hefty-ass fines of up to 20 million Euros or 4% of your annual global turnover. Whichever is higher.

As a designer, you actually need to know how things like the GDPR works. Because when your boss tells you to design something to collect users' email addresses, you need to ask why. That's your job. To be fair, that was *always* your job and if there's no good reason to be collecting those email addresses, you need to say no. You need to be more concerned about protecting people's data than in getting it in your boss' hands. As the defense against monsters—which I hope I've convinced you that you are by now—it's our job to make sure we're not mistreating the people who use services we design. The GDPR isn't an outlier. It's the first big step toward a more government-regulated internet. And we don't get to complain about it because we had an opportunity to regulate ourselves and we didn't. Even in the absence of regulations, safeguarding the people we design for is the job.

Let's not get regulations and ethics confused. Trafficking in private user data was as unethical before the GDPR as it is after. It's also now illegal. This is great, but plenty of legal activities are still unethical. For example, it's not illegal (yet) for Uber to keep tracking you once you get out of their car and go about your business. (As they do.) But we can agree that it's sketchy as fuck. And unethical. We're discovering new terrible things to do to society every day. It's gonna take the law time to catch up. (On some things they never will.) Until then, we're people's last line of defense. Pro tip: if your boss asks you to do something and says, "It's not *technically* illegal," it's probably unethical.

Let's talk about Twitter's German Nazi filter. Germany has strict laws banning Nazi symbols, incitement of the people, and hate speech, which they refer to as *Volksverhetzung* (incitement of the masses). This is because Germany is actually dealing with the atrocities committed on their soil, unlike the United States and slavery, Jim Crow, Native American genocide, etc. It's also illegal to deny the existence of the Holocaust in Germany. In June 2017, the complete Volksverhetzung laws expanded to include sweeping new regulations for social networks called the *Netzwerkdurchsetzungsgesetz*, or Network Enforcement Act . (Meanwhile, in Silicon Valley, on October 8, 2018, in an interview with Kara Swisher, Mark Zuckerberg specifically mentioned Holocaust deniers were welcome on his platform.) So, if you're doing business in Germany, you need a way to shut down the Nazi shit. Twitter, obviously, works in Germany. Twitter is also filled with Nazi shit. In order to operate in Germany, they needed a way to filter that hateful crap out. Which they figured out.

Try this: go to your Twitter content settings and change the country to Germany. The Nazis go away! It's the software equivalent of D-Day. Nazis gone. The next time Twitter tells you they don't know how to find the Nazi stuff, be assured they're lying. They've already had to tag it.

Why don't they turn it off worldwide? Great question. In fact, I asked Jack Dorsey that question in person. He said it's not illegal in the United States. It may not be illegal, but giving a voice to someone who uses it to silence others is indecent, unethical, and cruel. As designers, our job is to protect the people who come in contact with the tools we build. Sometimes the law can back us up, like with the GDPR. Sometimes the law may be lagging a little bit behind.

If this all sounds like more than you bargained for when you decided to become a designer, it may be. Yet here we are. No one prepared us for this. We're going to need thicker skins. We're going to need to care about things that didn't seem important before—which is maybe why we're in this mess to begin with. We're going to have to acknowledge our power to affect the things we design. And we're going to need to take a stand. If

Donald J. Trump
@realDonaldTrump

Describe the issue   Cancel

Help us understand the problem. What is going on with this
Tweet?

I'm not interested in this Tweet

It's spam

It's abusive or harmful

Covered by Netzwerkdurchsetzungsgesetz

Learn more about reporting violations of our rules.

anyone's still reading and thinking that the worst thing in the world is to get fired, let the lesson of James Liang soak over you...

We can go to jail for this shit now!

We are going to need to be better designers. To see how we do that, we need to look at how designers are made and at what they're taught. Cover your nose. Because design education stinks.

DESIGN EDUCATION STINKS

Before I start this section, let me acknowledge all the smart, kind, decent, caring people I know who work in design education. I am not here to tear down your good work. I know how much you care about your students and how criminally underpaid you are. My goal here is to help. I want to support what you are doing, I want you to have better facilities. I want you to have better tools. I want you to get paid what you're worth; and I love that you're educating the future practitioners of our craft. (Plus I may be coming to you for a job soon.)

Design education, with a few exceptions (you can pretend the school or program you went to is an exception if it makes you feel better about the student loans you're still paying off), is inherently broken.

How do I know this? I run a design studio.

I've been hiring designers for almost two decades. Whenever I post a design job, I end up interviewing two kinds of people: ones who went to design school, and ones who got into design through the side door. The ones who took the scenic route into design show up with degrees in poetry, English, Russian literature, computer science, journalism, and every other branch of the liberal arts tree. One of the best designers I ever worked with had a psychology degree. That wasn't an accident. The psychology degree was a major factor of what made him good at designing. What all of these people had in common was a well-rounded curiosity, the good sense to know when something wasn't working, and good social skills. Not only could they design well, they could write, think analytically; and they were curious about every job in the shop. If a job in the shop needed to be done, they'd volunteer to do it, even if (or maybe especially if) it meant having to learn a new skill.

Some of these folks made their switch to design by enrolling in programs like General Assembly and other boot camp type places that promise to teach you the principles of UX in ten weeks, or even—god help us all—in a one-week accelerated course[21]. While I was originally skeptical of programs like this (and still am for the most part), I'm supportive of the idea that there's a point of entry into the field for the designers of the future unable to pay for the increasingly hostile cost of a college tuition. I've also talked to a few instructors who teach at programs like this who've told me they cover ethics. (I'm sure there are also those that don't.) Many of the people enrolled in these programs are paying for it with their own money. Never underestimate the value of spending your own money. You're less inclined to waste it.

In contrast, almost every design school graduate I interviewed, while super-talented, lacked the basic core of what it takes to become a professional designer coming out of school. They lacked a basic understanding of how businesses work, how to research a problem, how to measure the impact of their work, how to present work effectively, and how to take criticism. Not to mention basic shit like how to charge for their work or write an invoice. More importantly, they seemed to lack a curiosity about these things. Once your sense of "what a designer is and does" is baked, and served up on a plate of student loans, it's really hard to change it. To grossly paraphrase Upton Sinclair, "It is difficult to get a person to understand something when they're making student loan payments on already understanding it."

In design school, professional practices are usually grouped together and referred to as "soft skills," taught in something called a "portfolio class" by whichever professor drew the short straw that semester. Unpacking professional practice is less glamorous than holding forth about creativity. To be fair, I doubt many high school seniors are excited to choose a design school based on how well they teach professional services. I certainly wasn't. We choose design schools based on how amazingly creative and special they make us feel. Bernard Roth, co-founder of Stanford's d.school, one of the most prestigious design schools in the world, put it this way:

"In the Stanford d.school we attempt to bring students through a series of experiences that change their self-image so that they think of themselves as being more creative. We call this boosting their creative confidence."

I call it boosting the likelihood these kids end up in jail. Today's design students don't need help with their self-image any more so than any other students. Creativity can't be the cornerstone of a design foundation anymore. We need to teach students the responsibilities of their craft, and it needs to be done at the foundational level. We need to value the consequences of our actions more than the cleverness of our ideas. As design educators, we need to stop pulling out a syllabus that was put together while watching the Nixon impeachment hearings, and we need to stop convincing students they're special unicorns immune to consequence. The School of Visual Arts says in one of their course descriptions: "We will create a space for your individual, unique art path."

Cool.

Allowing a twenty-year-old to amass $100K in debt without teaching them the skills they'll need to help pay off that debt is criminal. Learning how to earn a living practicing your craft is the bare minimum anyone should expect to get out of any education. Learning how to earn a living while practicing that craft ethically almost begins to justify the cost of that education. Almost. Learning how to practice that craft in a way that keeps designers out of jail, and society from burning down, is your new success metric for education.

Working ethically is a skill, and it's a skill that needs to be taught and then developed. It's not easy to tell the CEO of a Fortune 500 company that the product they just asked you to design is harmful. It takes more than guts. It takes knowing what questions to ask. It takes knowing how to test the effects of the product. It takes knowing how to build a good argument. And it takes seeing yourself as an equal stakeholder in the product. It takes seeing yourself as a defender. And frankly, it takes some designers who've come from backgrounds and experiences that were harmed by the products of Fortune 500 companies. It takes a lot. Design schools aren't training their students how to have those conversations. Designers aren't going to win these conversation while they see themselves as special creative unicorns.

I've interviewed design school graduates who couldn't write an introductory email, don't know how to talk about their work, who cried when I gave them feedback, who had too narrow a definition of design (I'll only do *these* things!), and who couldn't name three designers they admired. I've had design school graduates show up and apply for a job as if they were here to declare a major. If you're a design educator reading this and thinking, "well at least I taught them color theory," let me break it to you— no you did not. They didn't know that either.

The biggest problem, by far, is they confuse solving design problems with personal expression.

The vast majority of design programs across the world still live within art schools. Not to shit on art schools—they're a fine place to learn how to make art; but art has as much in common with design as a lobster has with a carrot cake. In 2019, there is simply no venn diagram where design schools and art schools overlap. I know this because I went to art school. I was taught how to be as creative as possible, how to explore my "passion," and how to glue broken plates to canvas. (It was the '90s). When you're teaching design in this environment, design students start believing those things apply to them as well. They don't.

Sure, there's a certain amount of creativity in design, but that's just one part of a very meaty, robust toolkit. Teaching a designer to be creative without teaching them ethics is akin to a medical school teaching a surgeon how to open up a torso without teaching them how internal organs work. Anyone who wants a career as a designer is going to need to speak about someone's business and organizational goals. They're going to have to learn how to analyze data, and how to measure effectiveness. They're going to have to learn how to build and extend brands and to do goal-driven work. Most of all, they need to learn how to measure the effectiveness of their own work. Not only for the company, but more importantly for society at large. Design is not about expressing yourself. Design is not about following your dream. Design is not about becoming a creative. Design is about keeping people from doing terrible things to other people.

There was a time in America when barbers did dental work, which basically meant pulling teeth. Dentistry has gotten more complex. There was a time when teaching design within art schools might've made sense. It usually meant graphic design, which is great, and maybe graphic design *should* remain in art school. I love graphic design! I still buy vinyl records because I love the covers. But when we're talking about interactive design, or UX design, or design thinking, or any other bullshit terms we'll make up in the next six months, we need to expand our curriculum by a *wide* margin.

Yes, I realize I am tarring an entire educational system with one large brush, and I'm sure there are exceptions to this rule, but they *are* exceptions. We have a responsibility to the craft, and the craft has a responsibility to society. A design education needs to build fierce designers who are not afraid to stand up to the people and companies they work with. We need to build designers who understand their job is not to be a pair of hands, but to be society's line of defense. We need to train designers who aren't afraid to ask why and say no.

The problem with design education is there's a nearly complete mismatch between education and professional practice. We're not teaching what needs to be taught. We're not teaching in the places where learning can happen. The design programs I've alluded to above are living in a fantasy world where they're promising students a complete education, but they're unable to provide it by themselves. We need to divide the burden of preparation among higher education institutions, on-the-job training— software companies who make the tools are a huge under-acknowledged source of design education to make up for what the schools aren't doing; and continuing professional education.

The problem with UX design as a field is that it's so relatively new that we're not sure how to teach it, but the consequences of getting it wrong are so massive. Training tomorrow's designers is a complex job, and we can't do it with yesterday's tools, in yesterday's schools. We need something new. By which I mean something that's already happening somewhere else, an educational program that handles people doing complex and dangerous work:

Let's talk about doctors again. They're fun. How do you become a doctor? Turns out you start by going to a pre-med program. That's going to be about four or five years of basic stuff. You learn things like chemistry, biology, math, physics, etc. The whole point of pre-med is to see if you can cut it and to prepare you for actually going to medical school. But before you can even apply for medical school you need to pass the MCAT (which is the GRE for doctors). Once you pass the MCAT, you can apply for medical school, which is not easy to get into. If you're lucky enough to get in, prepare yourself for another four years of intense study, but this time you get to stick your hands inside cadavers. Enjoy. Are you a doctor yet? Slow your roll, because it's time for your residency. Which, depending on what kind of specialty you choose, can last anywhere from three to seven years. Then you have to pass a test to get your medical license. Congratulations, now you're a doctor.

Now there are plenty of points in that ordeal where you can jump off. You can just do the premed stuff, and become a chemist, or get a job in a lab. You can take the short end of a residency, and go into family practice, or keep going to become a surgeon. And before you start thinking how difficult all that is, ask yourself whether you'd want someone who took a one week intensive class in "Bones! How do they even work?" resetting the arm you broke snowboarding. Turns out we like it when the people who take care of us have the training they need.

You know what part of your medical educational experience prepares you for what you want to do as a doctor. Design education could use that kind of clarity. The different levels of achievement work as checks and balances. Imagine needing two years of extra schooling and certification before you got near anything with data collection implications. Imagine having to do a residency of a few years before being given direct control of the tools. Imagine every fresh graduate doing a five-year paid apprenticeship, working for someone who could teach them how the job actually gets done. Sadly, you're more likely to see a lineup of luxury buses in the parking lot at graduation ready to take a fresh new crop of newly-minted designers to Google, or Amazon, or Facebook. They'll be offered dangerous jobs, given precious little training, and told to work at an alarming pace, and to be on call 24/7. They'll do what they're told. They'll make crap. Most of them will have short unhappy careers. But that's okay, because there's always a fresh batch of new graduates.

Having a successful design career has little to do with how creative you are. I've seen plenty of creative people's careers derail because they couldn't manage their shit. They couldn't present their work effectively. They couldn't speak about project goals. They couldn't elicit or respond to feedback. They didn't know to ask why, and they were afraid to say no. I want you to manage your shit. Because no matter how good a designer's work is, at some point they're going to have to have to stand in front of someone who can fire them and keep them from doing something stupid. That's the day you actually become a designer.

A few months ago, I was teaching an ethics workshop in New York, and I asked the participants how many of them had ever been fired from a design job. A couple of brave souls raised their hands. I think they thought they were in trouble. I told them I've been fired at least half a dozen times, as an employee and as part of a studio. Getting fired is stressful, granted. The trick to not being stressed out about getting fired is to expect it every day. Work toward it. Be willing to say the thing that might get you fired, because if you're not, then you're holding back. Otherwise, you're giving the answer you think people want to hear, or the answer that you think saves your skin. That's not the job. Your job is to design things the right way, the ethical way, even if it gets you fired. They should teach you *that* in design school. Especially now that the alternative might include going to jail.

Instead, they teach you how to make little gifts for clients so they remember you—which go right in the trash after you leave, by the way.

DESIGN HIRING IS BROKEN

Look at some design job listings and you'll find that they mostly fit into two categories: the first category is filled with words and phrases like *creative, follow your passion, bliss, express your vision, follow your dreams, ride a unicorn, explore your inner something-or-other, #lovewhereyouwork,* etc. Sadly, most of us left ~~art~~ design school believing these phrases describe what we do, so we end up applying for crap in that category.

The second category includes things like grinding at maximum speed, *rockstar, ninja, speed demon, crushing* and *busting* all manner of things, *interest in blockchain a major plus,* etc. That's the evolving language of tech, where moving fast and scaling quickly reigns supreme.

But don't take my word for it. Here's a few choice bits I found by wading into a job posting site for a brief ten minutes:

Quick to react when given new information, direction, and goals.

You never quit, never take no for an answer, and ultimately succeed in everything you do!

Be comfortable with ambiguity.

You'll need to be excited about working with incomplete information.

You're a magician, able to make deep science sexy and snackable.

And my personal favorite:

Ability to self-manage workload between multiple stakeholders.

That, dear reader, is how you describe a toilet.

This is the landscape of dumbfuckery that designers weed through when looking for a job.

The majority of young designers graduating from schools these days will end up thrown headfirst into a meat grinder, lured in by job descriptions like the ones above. Lured by promises of nurturing, collaboration, excitement, and kombucha on tap, they'll join a team with people who have roughly the same experience as they do, give or take a year. If they're lucky, their design manager might have a couple of years experience more than they do, and they're the design manager only because they're the last sucker standing after everyone from their hiring class quit. Leadership by attrition! If you're a woman in this situation, you probably also have to deal with your manager inviting you into his open relationship during the first week on the job. So, these young designers have gotten an incomplete education, where they didn't get taught how to work, then they got thrust into a workforce where no one is available to train them, and in two weeks, they'll be asked to design privacy settings for a social network with over two billion users where people have complex relationships with different friends and family groups that need to be protected and walled off from each other. And they'll be asked to do it fast. Hopefully fast enough that no one has time to ask any questions. Don't worry though, the CEO is almost 40 years old. Except he just gave an interview where he said he was cool with Holocaust deniers on the service. Fuck.

This is how we got to where we are now.

The history of UX design is, until very very very recently, the history of design as defined by other fields. UX design was defined first by engineers because, let's be fair, they're the ones who invented the internet. They were designing stuff before anyone calling themselves a designer ever showed up. I guarantee they didn't call it design. But design it was. I have no doubt that the first "designer" ever hired in Silicon Valley was hired to do a skin job. "We've built a thing. It looks like shit. Make it not look like shit." It's a bit like asking someone to turn a folding chair into a mid-century lounge chair. I can duct tape a pillow to the seat, but the actual opportunity to design any comfort into that chair is long past.

Engineers' definition of design—the people in the bunny hats who make the colors—is still widely accepted by a large majority of designers working in the field today. Unfortunately, it's a definition that's been accepted by designers as well. And perpetuated by anyone who claims the mantle of "creative," which is a self-loathing term that needs to be killed with fire.

The truth is that design, when it comes to digital products, is a team sport. Designing a complex tool well takes people from a lot of different fields. Be they engineers, strategists, developers, or yes, designers.

On March 1st, 2017, Jared Spool, who's been doing yeoman's work for design for the better part of forty years, tweeted out the following:

"Anyone who influences what the design becomes is the designer. This includes developers, PMs, even corporate legal. All are the designers."

Everything in that tweet is correct. Everyone who influences the final thing, be it a product or a service, is designing. Yet, if you were to click through and look at the replies to that tweet, what you'd see is the evisceration of Jared Spool in defensive bite-sized little vitriolic thoughts still covered with the spittle of ego. Even more sadly, it quickly turns into a discussion of titles. We are happy to give away all the responsibilities that come with the job, but please don't take our titles! I have seen designers argue for a week with a new employer about what their title will be, without sparing one breath to ask about their responsibilities.

Design is a verb, an act. Anyone is free to pick up the ball and run with it. If you're not doing the job you're being paid to do, you can't be upset when someone else starts doing it. You cannot *not* design. The early engineers of Silicon Valley were, in fact, designing things. James Liang was hired by Volkswagen as an engineer. This doesn't change the fact that he designed the tool that landed him in jail. Engineers design things all the time. What a professional designer brings to the act is intention. But in order to do that, the designer needs to behave intentionally. Designers are dead. Long live design.

THE AGE OF CREATIVES IS OVER

If we want to call ourselves designers, we need to be willing to take responsibility (or at least show up) for shaping the design process from start to finish, from snout to tail. Because regardless of whether we take the responsibility or not, it looks like we're going to get the blame. Which, quite honestly, is as it should be. And the consequences just got a little more serious.

We can't afford to rely on old methods of education. If you're a design student, you need to demand a design education that's going to prepare you for the actual problems you're going to face in your career. If you're a design educator, it's time to update your curriculum. Today's designers need to be systems thinkers, experts in regulation, collaborators, communicators, and fearless. We need to understand our job is to be advocates for the people who aren't in the room. We need to understand we have a greater responsibility to society than to the people who sign the checks.

The age of creatives is over. It led us to a garbage fire. The age of resistance to enshittification is at hand.

Yesterday's solitary geniuses need to make way for collaborators. We fought for a seat at the table, and now that we have it, we should talk to the other people seated there! It's time to take off the expensive headphones, move to the desk in the center of the room, and start taking the lead on how things in our organizations are designed. Today's designer needs to encourage collaboration between people with different skill sets and experiences. She includes the people who need to be included in the design process, especially the ones who've been excluded in the past. She does this with authority. With agency. With good communication. And with conviction.

We're going to be held accountable for our actions. We've been moving fast. We've been breaking things, sometimes on purpose, sometimes out of ignorance. The effects are the same. The things we're building are bigger than they used to be and they have more reach. At the scale we're working, when we fuck up, we don't just break code, we break people. We break relationships. We break civil discourse. The moment to slow down is here. I started this chapter with the story of a man who went to jail for following unethical orders. When this story hit the news last year, it made waves because it was an outlier. People generally haven't gone to jail for designing thing. Except that's changing. James Liang isn't an outlier. He's a canary in a coal mine. A few years ago I was giving a talk where I mentioned that we weren't too far away from designers being sent to jail. I wish I'd been wrong, but I'm not surprised I wasn't. We've been careless. We've been negligent. We're hurting people. And it's catching up to us.

If you're a creative person who enjoys expressing themselves and looking forward to a career of exploring your unique vision, or being a brand ambassador, you might think I'm trying to talk you out of becoming a designer. You'd be right.

But mostly, I want to keep you out of jail.

All the White Boys in the Room

On March 21, 2006, Jack Dorsey published the world's first tweet: "just setting up my twttr."

On July 22, 2018, Donald Trump tweeted: "To Iranian President Rouhani: NEVER, EVER THREATEN THE UNITED STATES AGAIN OR YOU WILL SUFFER CONSEQUENCES THE LIKES OF WHICH FEW THROUGHOUT HISTORY HAVE EVER SUFFERED BEFORE. WE ARE NO LONGER A COUNTRY THAT WILL STAND FOR YOUR DEMENTED WORDS OF VIOLENCE & DEATH. BE CAUTIOUS!" *(Capitalization his.)*

In the twelve years between those two tweets, some things happened that are worth exploring. But first, let's explore what happened before that very first tweet was even sent, because it laid the foundation of everything that was to come later.

Twitter and my design shop, Mule, used to be right across the hall from each other in a run-down shitbox of a building in San Francisco's SOMA district. We were friends with a lot of the original crew that built the platform. They wanted to build a tool that let people communicate with each other easily. They were a decent bunch of guys—and that was the problem.

They were a bunch of guys. More accurately, they were a bunch of white guys. Those white guys, and I'll keep giving them the benefit of the doubt, and say they did it with the best of intentions, designed the foundation of a platform that would later collapse under the weight of harassment, abuse, death threats, rape threats, doxxing, and the eventual takeover of the alt-right and their racist idiot pumpkin king.

All the white boys in the room, even with the best of intentions, will only ever know what it's like to make decisions as a white boy. They will only ever have the experiences of white boys. This is true of anyone. You will design things that fit within your own experiences. Even those that attempt to look outside their own experiences will only ever know what questions to ask based on *that* experience. Even those doing good research can only ask questions *they* think to ask. In short, even the most well-meaning white boys don't know what they don't know. That's before we even deal with the ones that *aren't* well-meaning. (I see you, Travis.)

Twitter never built in a way to deal with harassment because none of the people designing it had ever been harassed, so it didn't come up. Twitter didn't build in a way to deal with threats because none of the people designing it had ever gotten a death threat. It didn't come up. Twitter didn't build in a way to deal with stalking because no one on the team had ever been stalked. It didn't come up. That's not to say those things don't happen to white boys. They do, but very rarely.

The prevailing wisdom of that era was that you built the tool you and your team wanted to use. You'd sometimes hear this phrased as "eating your own dog food." Charming. The problem is that when your team all have roughly the same experiences, and you end up building the tool that works for that team, you've marginalized everyone else.

Did I say prevailing wisdom of *that* era? I shit you not, as I'm writing that paragraph, my wife Erika Hall sends me this tweet:

"I've reviewed thousands of products. Without fail, it's the products built by people for themselves that continue to win. Why? When you

are the customer you don't have to guess what people want. Customer focus, incentive clarity & a razor sharp point-of-view creates great product."

That's from Brian Norgard, Chief Product Officer at Tinder, also an investor in SpaceX and Lyft. Sent out on July 25, 2018. The idea that you build the product you want to use is alive and well in Silicon Valley. (As is the idea that guesswork is the alternative to bravado.) Product teams in Silicon Valley are dominated by white males. (According to The National Center for Women & Information Technology's Women In Tech 2016 report[22], only twenty-five percent of computing jobs are held by women. The majority of those jobs are held by white women. Latinx women clocked in at one percent of that particular workforce.) That means not only are we excluding everyone who's not white and male (gonna go out on a crazy limb here and include heterosexual and cis in that description) from designing and building the tools of the future, we're *explicitly* excluding them from being served by those tools. We are white men building tools for white men.

For ten years, Twitter has been dealing with harassment and abuse on its platform. It's gone through a few CEOs. All white. All male. Every time there's a high profile attack, one of those CEOs comes out and does a dog and pony show about how Twitter will now finally—no really this time for real—actually look into cutting down abuse and then three weeks later, they roll out rounded corners for tweets instead. (I guess the tweets won't hurt as much now that the corners aren't so sharp?)

Previously, we've discussed how Twitter doesn't deal with harassment and abuse because they don't want to. Remember our Upton Sinclair quote. It's going to serve us well throughout this book: *It is difficult to get a man to understand something when his salary depends upon his not understanding it.*

But there's another reason. The second reason is that Twitter is too hard to fix. Twitter was broken from conception. Twitter's original sin occurred the day that four white boys sat around a room and designed the seed of what the platform would be. Having one very narrow singular viewpoint for a tool that ended up having a global reach was akin to building a time bomb within the foundation. As Twitter grew, it became harder and harder to go back and fix the foundation that was now propping up a towering inferno of garbage. At this point, abuse and harassment are as much a part of the Twitter experience as retweets and faves.

The idea that every voice is worth being amplified is core to Twitter's philosophy. Theoretically, I agree with that, but when theory hits reality, the results aren't always pretty. Because the reality is that some of those voices are using their augmentation to silence others. When you use your augmented right to question someone else's right to live, love, and/or pray as they see fit—you lose the right to that augmentation. While Twitter bends over backward to protect the voices that silence others, I believe that our job as designers, and as human beings, is to use our skills to protect the voices that are most in need of protection. When you use your voice to question someone else's humanity, you forfeit yours.

We have to be ready for any tool we build to have a global impact. But even if it only impacts the area around you, chances are it is going to, hopefully, reach people who are different from you. People who have different needs, different abilities, different cultures, different languages, different experiences, different tastes. Don't you want all of those people using your tool? Don't you want them to be able to participate in what you're making? And don't you want it to work for them? And, for the capitalists who might still be reading: don't you want their money? If we intend to build successful tools, we need to expand our definition of *we*.

OH YOU MUST BE TALKING ABOUT EMPATHY

Fuck no, I am not. I am talking about hiring. To paraphrase Google Sydney's Tea Uglow, why teach people to think outside the box when you can *hire* people outside the box. The last thing I want you to do is take your team of white boys out into the field and "see what the women think." Turns out women like to work. Turns out they've been dying to work in this field. Turns out they're willing to work in this field, even when it means putting up with all the bullshit men like me have thrown at them on a daily basis and then being paid seventy cents on the dollar. Turns out they're good at this work. Turns out they used to *own* this field! As Claire L. Evans writes in her excellent book *Broad Band*:

> *Before a new field developed its authorities, and long before there was money to be made, women experimented with new technologies and pushed them beyond their design. Again and again, women did the jobs no one thought were important, until they were.*

So, as it turns out, this was their field to begin with. We pushed them out when we saw there was glory to be had, then did a lot of hard work erasing their history and keeping them out of the field by convincing subsequent generations they couldn't do the job.

I'm going to be very honest with you here. This is the hardest chapter of the book to write. I'm part of the problem I'm describing. While I'm making a conscious effort to be more aware of my own biases, there are things I just don't know. Every door in this industry opens for me by default—well, maybe not after this book. I have to work half as hard to achieve twice as much as a woman or a person of color in this industry. That's not because I'm more talented or work harder or am smarter. It's because people look at me and see a person that matches what their idea of a designer looks like. They look at me, and decide I can be in the room. What I have achieved is not fully earned. Personally, I like to earn things. I wanna know that when I got a job it was because I beat *everyone*, not just the people you allowed in the room. I think that's what everyone is looking for here, a fair shot at earning their place. A *fair* shot. That means a woman doesn't have to work twice as hard to earn seventy cents on the dollar that some dude name Chad is making.

So, let everyone in the room.

Why should you listen to me? You shouldn't. You should listen to all the women out there telling you their stories of harassment in the workplace. You should listen to all the Black people who can't get inside the door because they're not a "culture fit." If you're lucky enough that this industry was built in your image, realize how lucky you are.

I sent an early draft of this chapter to Ani King, the editor of *Syntax & Salt* magazine. She's a friend, who works in the tech industry as an IT manager. After reading the draft, she felt compelled to share the following. It states the problem better than I could ever hope to:

> *A few years ago I was on a panel for MICWIC (Michigan Women in Computing), and the thing that struck me is how almost every single woman who spoke felt compelled to state that they "didn't hate men," as a measure of self protection, or say something that in some way excused behavior (it was the times, etc.)*

> *And some of these people were saying that they stayed in tech and engineering DESPITE feeling like they were unwanted the whole time, but that in some cases, they would never ask their other, bright, amazing female colleagues to come work with them, because they knew it was asking a lot.*

Until you let everyone in the room, until you give everyone a chance, you do not get to say you've earned *anything* in this business. At least not fairly. As long as you're the beneficiary of sexist, ableist, and racist hiring practices, you didn't earn that job. It was handed to you. And don't come to me complaining about quotas when "hire the white guy" is the biggest quota program in history.

MY FIRST DESIGN JOB

I got my first design job shortly after graduating from college. Mind you, while I'd taken a couple of design classes, I graduated with a degree in Fine Arts. (See again the previous chapter for how this happens.) It honestly wasn't so much a design job as a job "designing things" at the desktop publishing department at a copy shop. (Ask your parents.) It was the '90s. And while it wasn't a *great* job, it paid more than the job I previously had. Here's the thing; I wasn't qualified for it.

I remember looking at the job posting and thinking "I can't do a bunch of this stuff." I also remember thinking that I could learn. To be fair, I went out and got myself a copy of Mavis Beavis Teaches Typing (again, ask your parents) and spent the weekend learning how to type, because one of the requirements was typing eighty-five words per minute. Which I *still* can't do. Just ask my editor. I bought a couple of software manuals, and skimmed through them as well.

When the interview rolled around, I weaved and dodged through the questions, figuring I could learn all of this stuff as needed. (And I eventually did.) I tried not to sweat too much. I made eye contact. Again, it was a desktop publishing job. I was going to be laying out flyers and business cards, doing the occasional logo. But I lied about my skills and I got the job.

For years, I used to tell this story as a lesson in hustle and confidence. It isn't. It's a story about privilege. It's a story about the world being made in my favor. I knew about half the stuff I needed to know to walk into that interview. Chances are, the interviewer wasn't stupid. They probably realized I didn't know my shit, but there was something about me that convinced the interviewer to take a chance. I like to think it was my sparkling personality and probably a bit of it was. And probably a bit of it was that the interviewer looked across the table at me and saw someone that looked like them.

"If you are white in a white supremacist society, you are racist. If you are male in a patriarchy, you are sexist."

That quote is from Ijeoma Oluo's *So You Want To Talk About Race*, which I encourage you all to read. Especially if you look like me. (Look at the author photo on the back for a clue.) I am both those things. If you are reading this and you look like me, you are too. Regardless of how well you've lived your life, regardless of how good your intentions were, you've benefited from a stacked deck. When I walked into that interview, the person across the table was inclined to *want* to believe me. I was halfway there. A woman walking into that room has to do work I don't have to do. Twice as much. A Black or Latinx man walking into that situation has to do work that I don't have to do. Thrice as much. A Black or Latinx woman walking into that room probably doesn't stand a chance.

I can't be sure that I wouldn't have gotten the job if I was a woman or Black , but I can tell you without hesitation that I had a better chance of getting it because I was a white male. For one, not being qualified gave me zero pause. I saw a list of requirements, a few looked familiar, and I decided that was enough. That's privilege at work.

I've never walked into a room and had an interviewer wonder if I deserved to be there. Whether I consider myself a racist or a sexist, I have *absolutely* benefited from the tainted fruits of both racism and sexism. Undeniably. I don't think the interviewer on the other side of the table was racist or sexist except that, like myself, they'd benefitted from being born a white male.

UNCONSCIOUS BIAS

I'm under no pretense that this book can change the minds of the truly odious. (Sorry, Mr. Thiel.) While those people are most definitely a problem, they're not the biggest problem or the biggest opportunity for lasting change. That resides in the juicy middle, the majority of our industry, people like me and you who've been living our lives with unconscious bias.

For those of you not familiar with the term, I'll sum it up this way: it's all the little things we do, almost without thinking, that undermine the people around us who don't look like us. The classic example being when we ask the only woman in the meeting to take notes. Or when four white male engineers decide a Black female applicant just wouldn't be a good culture fit. (So many crimes are committed under the label of "culture fit" that it's not even funny.) Or when your team decides to celebrate a product launch by going to a strip club and the female designer feels weird about it, but doesn't wanna be a spoilsport, so she goes and has a horrible time and then everyone feels weird—and you solve the problem by not hiring any more women because you're a genius. Actually, that last one may not be unconscious bias as much as just being a straight-up asshole.

I teach a workshop in presenting work with confidence. In fact, it's called "Presenting Work with Confidence." Clever. The unofficial secret name for the workshop is "Teaching Women to Speak Up and Teaching Men to Shut Up." I've been teaching this workshop for three years and counting. I've taught it in the States, Canada, Europe, Australia, and India. I tell you this without reservation: men have no problem interrupting women all over the world. We absolutely suck at it, me included. You're probably thinking, like I have many times, "Sure, but it's not because I'm a guy. It's because I'm me." Let me reassure you, it's because you're a guy. Because throughout the workshop, I'll keep my eye on the dudes interrupting women and they're not interrupting the men who come up to present.

There's no quicker way to destroy someone's confidence than teaching them that what they're saying isn't as important as what *you're* saying.

Everyone earned the right to be heard at work when you hired them, and not only do they have the right to be heard, you're an idiot for not listening to what they have to say! Here's an opportunity to hear from someone with a different viewpoint than yours and you're silencing them? What are you afraid of? That they'll tell you you're wrong? Hosanna in the highest and St. Joan of Arc be praised. That's exactly what you should be hoping for! Be thankful for the employee that will tell you that while you have a chance to do something about it.

If you're a dude, you have a responsibility to tell your male co-workers to shut the fuck up when they interrupt someone. Be a role model. I don't mean "I think what Rebecca was saying was—" I mean you should say "You interrupted Maria. I want to hear her finish." Not because I think Maria needs saving, but because it's important for the other guys in the room to see that this is not longer tolerated by their own.

This is the shit we have to watch out for. The little crap. Interrupting women. Deciding you're hip enough to use racial slang with a Black co-worker. (Shut up. You know exactly what I'm talking about.) Telling a coworker she looks hot. Telling her to smile more. "Are you on Tinder?" Speaking in racial dialects at work. (Let's finally admit that Apu's voice was always racist and just stop.) Holding off-sites at bars. "Where are you *really* from?" Scheduling all-night hack-a-thons that coworkers with children can't (or frankly, just don't *want)* to participate in. This is the shit we say and do without thinking twice. We may even be stupid enough to think some of it is complimentary. (I'm guilty of that.) But it's not. It sucks to deal with.

You know how much stuff you have to do on a regular day? Imagine your hardest day at work, on deadline, tons of shit to do, barely keeping on top of it. Now, imagine you have to do all that, along with monitoring the shit your coworkers are saying about you—the looks they're giving you—the little jabs here and there—not being allowed to finish your sentences—having someone take credit for your ideas. You couldn't do it, so stop putting that kind of burden on others.

And for the love of god, don't ask to touch your Black coworkers' hair.

BETTER HIRING

A few weeks ago, a good friend of mine was looking to hire someone for his company. He wanted to make sure women would apply for this job. (Hold on a second, I need to deal with the libertarians right now: there's absolutely nothing illegal or unethical in tailoring a job description to entice more women to apply. In fact, it should be a goal. Now, wipe your man tears away, get your mom to make you a nice cup of warm milk or a Hot Pocket and keep reading.) Anyway, this friend of mine is in our secret Slack channel, and the women in the channel are giving him advice on how to write that application based on their own experiences applying for jobs, and in some cases, writing job descriptions themselves. (Women can be bosses, too!)

Their suggestions were to write the job description so that it emphasized the work they'd be doing; to talk about the people they'd be working with, the community they'd be joining, and why that work was important to be doing. They suggested talking about how this hire would be complementing an already great team. They suggested emphasizing the company's goals rather than individual achievement, and how rather than saying things like "you need five years experience doing x," you're better off with "be ready to discuss how your previous experiences can help us do x". Because let's face it, it's hard to get five years of experience doing something when you work in an industry that won't hire you to do it.

Compare that to your standard startup job description looking for "a rockstar who's been crushing code for five years in a high-powered environment and isn't afraid to knock heads." *I* don't want to work at that company! So imagine what it's like for a woman or a minority to read a job description like that, then Google the company's About Us page and see a bunch of bros staring back at them. We get the job applicants we deserve. Today's design isn't done by rock stars. It isn't done by ninjas, and it isn't done by solo supermen. It's done by teams who know how to work together, to look at a problem from multiple points of view and a diverse set of experiences. So, let's stop writing job descriptions to appeal to solitary boy geniuses with hero's journey damage—and start hiring grownups.

OUR DIVERSITY IS OUR STRENGTH

Let me tell you an embarrassing story. (I have many, by the way.) Remember those ten ethics points I made a few chapters back? Well, this book first started as a little booklet that I made for designers and I made a little one-page website for that booklet. At the same time, I had the idea of asking a few designers and illustrators to make posters of the ten points. I wanted lots of different styles so people could find one that spoke to them. I made sure at least half of the posters were made by women, who were gracious enough to make them. When I announced the site, via a tweet, I made a point that half the posters were by women. I was really proud of that. (But let's face it—I was also virtue signaling.)

Within five minutes of that tweet, someone replied that I'd included no Black people at all. I was furious. Here I was doing something for the good of the community, and some little shit comes along and pees all over it. Except they were right. There were no posters in the collection from people of color. It might as well have been sponsored by Cracker Barrel. As embarrassing as that was, I compounded it with my initial reaction of anger. I'm pretty sure I tweeted back something incredibly defensive. Of course, in hindsight the person I was mad at was myself. I was mad I didn't see it. Was I consciously attempting to leave people of color out of the project? Of course not, but the effect is the same, and that's the thing to focus on. We could argue about my intent, but that makes it about me. Whether by action or inaction, whether by malice or blind spot, there were no Black people in the project. They'd been marginalized once again. It was racist.

The people affected by our actions are always more important than our intent.

Twitter didn't intend to build the perfect tool for harassment and abuse. Airbnb didn't intend to build a racist housing market. Facebook didn't intend to endanger trans people with their Real Names project. (In fact, they thought they were solving abuse and harassment on their platform.) Just like I didn't intend to leave people of color out of my poster project. But all those things happened, intentionally or not, because in each of those cases, those services were created by a bunch of people with the same skin tone, the same gender, the same educational experience (more or less), and the same backgrounds (more or less). I have no doubt that if I'd been working with a person of color on that poster project, they would've seen what I didn't. I have no doubt that had there been a trans person on the Facebook RealNames project, they would've seen the problem with that initiative. I have no doubt that had there been a woman on the initial Twitter team, they would've asked "What do we do when creeps show up?"

In fact, I posed this very scenario to Heather Champ, who for years headed up Flickr's Trust and Safety team. We were discussing how it took Twitter a year to add the ability to block other users on the platform. I asked her how long it would've taken if she'd been on the team and, without missing a beat, she replied "it wouldn't have launched without it."

You put people from different backgrounds together, and they can see things from multiple points of view. They cover each others' blind spots. It's the smart move.

Oh, this is probably the point at which the white boy libertarians are screaming that I'm not backing up my assertions that diversity helps us build better products with any data. "Show me the data!" they like to scream. Okay, here it is: you jackasses have been running the world for millennia and it's a garbage fire. You've been running Silicon Valley for decades, and it's a Nazi-filled viper's nest. There's your data. You fucked it up. Also, this is an ethics book. We don't exclude people from working because allowing people to work is the right thing to do. We give everyone a chance to help because it's the right thing to do. We build products with everyone in mind because it's the right thing to do. But since we're talking about data, I'd be happy to see the data that supports excluding other people from the workforce based on race, gender, or religious beliefs.

People aren't arguing for inclusion. It's only inclusion from the white boys' side of the fence. For everyone else, it's exclusion. So, rather than asking me for data, let me ask you why you're okay excluding people who don't look like you. Better yet, ask yourself that every day. That's how we get better.

My friend Steph Monette has been working as an engineer in Silicon Valley for nine years. She's very good at her job, but despite that, she tells me she still has recruits attempting to get her to accept entry-level jobs until she "proves herself" on the job. I recently talked to her about her experience as a female engineer in various startups:

> *"It's exhausting. You work twice as hard as a lot of the guys do and you don't get as much recognition for it. I hope that people will learn the lessons from like everything that happened at Uber and things like that, but I think it's going to take a while for the impact to actually come through."*

TIME FOR ALLIES TO DIE

In February of 2018, I was in Copenhagen giving a new talk. I get nervous with new talks, not because public speaking makes me nervous, but because you never know whether a new talk sucks or not until you've given it a couple of times. You don't even really know what the talk is about until you've given it a few times. It wasn't until I was in the middle of this talk, which was ostensibly about ethics, that I realized it had a strong undercurrent of death throughout. Maybe undercurrent isn't the right word. It's quite possible that if you asked someone in the audience what the talk was about they would have replied, "death. That was some dark shit."

Later that evening, I went out to dinner with a couple of friends. We went to a place that specialized in "Nordic," which I assumed meant eating whale and drinking mead while *Thor: Ragnarok* played on a giant screen above the bar. It ended up being a very nice cozy place, with an even nicer owner. The kind of guy who grabs a bottle of bourbon, pulls up a chair for himself, and proceeds to tell you about spending ten years in the Danish military. In between stories of Finns building saunas in Kabul, and Americans taking their guns everywhere including the can, the topic of "being good allies" came up. To which my new Danish friend shouted that men our age had committed too many sins and done too many things wrong to ever be good allies in any sense of the word. The best thing we could do for the planet was to die.

Just a week before sitting down to write this, I watched as American school children walked out of school in protest after a school shooting. Because they're tired of going to school and getting shot. Because they're tired of their government caring more about fleecing their own pockets than comprehensive gun control. Because they're tired of their classes being interrupted to practice active shooter drills—and more than a few of them are tired of actually burying their classmates. As I'm watching these brave, brave kids, I'm filled with equal amounts of hope for the courage they're displaying and shame that our generation has left this problem for them to solve. We're a year away from the twentieth anniversary of the

Columbine High School massacre. We should've taken care of it then and there, before these brave kids were even born.

I start thinking that maybe my Danish ex-military friend is right. The best thing we can do for this planet is die.

My generation of designers had an amazing opportunity to make the world better than it was when it was handed to us, and it's becoming more and more apparent that we botched the job a thousandfold. We didn't make it better. We made it significantly worse.

Non-authoritarian societies are not made up of laws as much as they're made up of an agreement to follow those laws. While laws are delivered to us in a top-down fashion, the agreement to follow those laws is upheld from the bottom-up. A code of ethics will not magically transform us into people who behave decently. Its imposition, coming from the top, will have no transformative power. Only an agreement to follow it, made at the rank and file level, can change how we work.

This is where my hope comes from. I believe the people coming up after us will do a better job than we did. I believe that, as a 51-year-old white male living in America, my job is to clear the path for the voices I've silenced either knowingly or unknowingly. I cannot be a good ally because I've benefitted too much from the world I was born into. Regardless of whether I wanted those benefits or not, I got them.

I'll say it again: I am both racist and sexist, because I've benefited from both racism and sexism. If you are reading this and you look like me, you are those things too. Regardless of how well you've lived your life, regardless of how good your intentions were, you benefited from a stacked deck. Yet, even with the deck stacked in our favor, we couldn't do the job. So yes, the best thing we can do for the planet is to die.

Death is always a given. It is not a choice. We're all automatically enrolled in this program right from birth. As a culture, we spend a lot of time attempting to delay it or comically convincing ourselves it's not coming. But there's absolutely nothing we can do to stop it. Death. Is. Coming. Rather than spend a lifetime convincing ourselves that it's not, and wasting our energy attempting to outrun it, perhaps we are better served in attempting to earn it. As the great James Baldwin puts it, "It seems to me that one ought to rejoice in the fact of death—ought to decide, indeed, to earn one's death by confronting with passion the conundrum of life."

Perhaps, just perhaps, the point of life is to earn the death that comes at the end. And perhaps, no—*most likely*, that death is best earned by doing everything we can for those coming up after us. Earn your death by making room for the generation behind you. Might they fuck it up as well? Of course. But you already have. They still have a chance.

Here's the thing. When I look out over the horizon at everything white boys have built while they were in charge, I don't see good things. I see harassment and abuse. I see the re-emergence of Nazis. (You idiots let Nazis come back! Killing Nazis was one of the few things you used to be able to point to with pride!) I see racism going mainstream. I see Elon Musk using Twitter to call a rescue worker a pedophile. I see women leaving the workforce in droves. (According to a report by The Center for Talent Innovation[23], women are forty-five percent more likely to leave a tech job after a year than a man.) I certainly don't see the kind of results that would make anyone wanna sign up for another two thousand years of white boy leadership. We had everything going in our favor. We had to work half as hard as anyone else. We got all the breaks, and we still set the world on fire.

We don't get to stand in front of the raging dumpster fire we created and ask for a medal.

PART TWO

What We Can Do to Fix It

"Do you see over yonder, friend Sancho, thirty or forty hulking giants? I intend to do battle with them and slay them."

— Miguel de Cervantes, Don Quixote

Choosing Where to Work

Shortly after the 2016 Presidential election, I found myself at a meetup for tech people wanting to help nonprofits.

Like many people across the country, these people were looking for some way to make a difference. It was a seriously commendable endeavor. I applaud the people who threw it, and the people who attended it, but since I'm about to dump ice water on their dreams, I won't mention their names. I'm sure everyone involved meant well—and they're certainly more commendable than people who ain't doing shit. As people went around the room discussing where they worked and why they were there, I heard a lot of guilt. "I work at Uber, so it feels good to be doing this." It wasn't the sound of people looking to do further good work, it was the sound of people ashamed of what they do during the day.

Here's the thing. You can't help Uber build Greyball during the day, help Palantir design databases to round up immigrants, or work at a social network that helps Alex Jones amplify his onerous lies, and then buy ethics offsets by doing a nonprofit side hustle. We need you to work ethically during that day job much more than we need you working with that nonprofit evenings and weekends.

You can't make up for the terrible things you do at your day job with ethics offsets. If you want to truly do good work, you're better off applying your ethical framework to your day job. If you *really* feel bad about what you're doing at Palantir, go change what's happening at Palantir.

Ethics cannot be a side hustle.

Over the years, I've had a lot of designers ask me, "where can I do good work?" and they don't mean *good* as in quality. They mean good as in *on the side of the angels*. They look at the world, and they see a garbage fire. They wanna help put it out. That's commendable. If there's been a shred of a silver lining in our industry lately, it's seeing people thinking about the ramifications of their work. It gives me a glimmer of hope. Again, I wouldn't be writing this book if I didn't think there was hope.

Where can you do good work? The answer is so obvious as to be painful. Are you at work right now? Stand up. Look around. See those weird people putting post-its on the wall? See that kid in the corner desk whose headphones cost the annual GDP of a small nation? See the people typing away on various things? They're all doing work. Which means, with a few exceptions, the work they're doing has the possibility of being done right, as long as the people doing it take the right approach. The best place to do good work is right there where you are standing.

Doing good work isn't a matter of location. It's a matter of craft and a matter of responsibility.

If you want to do good work, start doing it at your day job. Start asking questions about what you're building. Start asking questions about who benefits from what you're building. Start asking questions about who gets hurt by what you're building. Take a look at your team. Does it look like the audience you're trying to reach? Especially if you're building something in the social sphere, where trust, safety, and understanding the needs of a diverse audience is paramount.

Ask your managers these questions as well. If you're not satisfied with their answers, stop designing. Continue asking questions until you get those answers. Designing something without understanding the ramifications of what it does is as unethical as designing something you know to be harmful.

But, won't somebody else make it? I get this question a lot too. The answer is yes. They might. And holy shit, that can make you feel powerless. But here's the thing: just because the person next to you might be an asshole, it's not a good excuse for you to be one. I get that you don't want to lose your job, and I get that you have rent to pay, but earning your living at the expense of someone else's livelihood, or life, is not a good way to live.

So, rather than asking yourself "won't somebody else make it?" ask yourself "what if me saying no is the inspiration for other people to stand up? What if me saying no is the first step in a movement? What if me saying no is the first step to making things right?"

We can debate whether tech or design are neutral in nature for weeks. It's a conversation I look forward to. (The answer is no, by the way.) But whether you think they are or not, I know that people are not neutral. You cannot afford to be neutral. Right now, more than ever, you need to reach down deep into your core, find your ethical strength, and bring it to your day job with you every day.

Then we can talk about helping nonprofits in the evening. Hurry up, because they do need your help.

THE MYTH OF SOCIAL IMPACT

I was having dinner with a designer friend not too long ago. She was feeling done with her job. For the last few years, she's been working at a large tech company. She was advancing within the company, doing well, being respected by colleagues, working on far-reaching projects. But she wasn't feeling it anymore. It happens.

"What do you feel like doing next?"

"Something with social impact."

"The shit your team designs affects two billion people. That has a massive social impact."

"I fucking hate you."

She stayed. Was she able to effect positive change within that company? Unclear. Large ships turn slowly. At least I knew there was someone who wanted to create positive social impact, and knew how to do it, working in a place that needed it.

We have everything backward right now. We've got the people with the least amount of experience, sometimes fresh out of school, making decisions at the largest platforms in the world. Services that affect billions of people. Services that need to understand the effects of their decisions on multitudes of communities. Services where we share our most intimate thoughts and our most private information. Meanwhile, the workers with the most experience in dealing with this stuff are burning out and going off to do work at nonprofits and NGOs.

Again, those places need the help. Some of them are doing things as close to holy work as our society can manage. I also understand being burned out, but at this particular moment in time, we need our best people where the biggest problems live. We need our best people in a position to tell Jack Dorsey to go fuck himself. We need people at Facebook who see themselves as resistance against monsters. We need people who are willing to look at a product lead and say, "I will absolutely, under no circumstances, build a tool to share our users' banking data, relationship data, or medical data." We need our strongest fighters in position to fight against hate speech at Twitter. An inexperienced designer fresh out of school has neither the experience, nor the skill to do any of those things, as willing as they might be. Worst yet, when they go to work at those places, there's no one there to train them on how to argue, how to ask questions, how to stand up for themselves, how to look out for the impact of their work.

So if you want to do work with social impact, and I honestly cannot believe I'm saying this, but it's absolutely true—we need you at places like Facebook. But we need you with swords drawn. We need you going there to fight. Facebook is either here for a long time; in which case it needs to be fixed, or it's falling apart, in which case it needs to be imploded carefully. Facebook data is like plutonium rods. If Facebook falls, it needs to be disposed of carefully and with intent.

But in its current form, and under its current leadership, Facebook is doing a fuckton of damage, not just to the users within the platform, but to society in general. We just saw Facebook get duped into influencing an election. Anyone who saw Mark Zuckerberg speaking to Congress on April of 2018 realizes that if there's any hope for intelligent thought within that organization, it doesn't sit at the top. It sits with the rank and file. It sits with the layer of management directly above the rank and file. These are layers you can get hired into! Go to Facebook and, in the words of the great John Lewis, make good trouble!

I happen to know several people who work at Facebook. (Whether they're still there when you're reading this book is another matter.) They're honestly trying to do good work there, and they understand what happens if they can't. That's why most of our conversations happen over drinks. Most of our conversations include them saying some variation of "I can't get [noun] to care about [verb]." And as easy as it is to make fun of people who want to "change things from the inside,"—I'm guilty of this myself and will continue to do it in the very next section!—I do believe these particular people mean it. They feel an actual responsibility to protect us from the monsters beyond the wall. They're the fucking Night's Watch! And like the actual Night Watch, they need reinforcements because they're at ground zero for where the real attack is coming from. There's something worthy in that. (Also, I'm gonna finish my book before George R.R. Martin finishes his.)

Obviously, Facebook's not the only company that meets those criteria, but they're certainly one of the biggest. If you're serious about making a social impact, your first question should be where are people getting screwed the most? Financial services. The medical industry. Education. Civil services. (Your city needs you!) The list is pretty long. Your second question should be whether you can keep people from getting screwed by working there. And if that answer is yes, that's where we need you to fight. Obviously, the answer to the second question is only partially up to you. Your desire to change things from the inside is only possible when a company is open to being changed. Very few companies want to change. Especially if what they're doing is working out financially, if not socially. Change is hard. You're going to have to fight people who are benefitting from the way things are being run. Therein lies the third question: Am I working at a place where I can actually change things?

CHANGING THINGS FROM THE INSIDE

On August 7th, 2018, Jack Dorsey tweeted out an explanation of why Twitter wasn't banning Alex Jones or his show, InfoWars, from its service:

We didn't suspend Alex Jones or Infowars yesterday. We know that's hard for many but the reason is simple: he hasn't violated our rules. We'll enforce if he does. And we'll continue to promote a healthy conversational environment by ensuring tweets aren't artificially amplified.

This was on the heels of Apple, Google, YouTube, Pinterest, Spotify, and yes, even YouPorn, banning him from their platforms. Jack's explanation itself was a challenge of comprehension. In fact, tech journalist Kara Swisher described his rumblings as "the high-minded tone that one takes with small children" in an opinion piece published in the New York Times the next day.

I've known plenty of people who've worked at Twitter over the years, some who were there from the beginning. I've watched as they've gone from being very happy to be working at a platform that was uniting people, to being concerned the platform had some problems, to being worried the concerns they were voicing weren't being taken seriously, to freaking out their company was now a megaphone for white supremacists. I've watched as people exhausted themselves in trying to change the direction of the company to no avail. Eventually, their declarations that they were

This person is changing things from the inside.

"changing things from the inside" weren't ringing true anymore. Most of the people I knew there have now left. All of them telling a version of the same story: "I tried hard to change things. It's not possible." Those that remained have turned defensive. They hung in too long.

You can change a company that's afraid of change. You can change a company that finds change uncomfortable. You cannot change a company that doesn't want to change, especially when leadership doesn't want to change. Here's a good tell: a good leadership team will generally be more open to change than the rank and file—after all, they're all wearing golden parachutes— even in cases where they need convincing. A good leadership team will ultimately get it. But a leadership team that sees itself driving into a burning forest and hits the accelerator, as Twitter is doing, can't be saved. At which point, you need to get out of there before you're complicit in what they're doing.

As Jack Dorsey was tweeting out a defense of Alex Jones, one of their employees, who was publicly towing the company lines, was DMing my wife, who has a large Twitter following, asking her to retweet tweets critical of their official position. If you're passing notes to the people on the outside, you're not changing things from the inside. You're a hostage.

At this point, everyone at Twitter is complicit in what they're doing.

OKAY, TWITTER ASIDE, CAN GOOD WORK BE DONE ANYWHERE THEN?

Nope.

Previously, we've discussed ethical ideas, executed unethically. That's a bucket I'd put almost all of the problematic companies we've discussed so far. Twitter. Uber. Facebook. Airbnb. All of these companies could've been run well and good work could've been done inside of them. In some cases, the companies were driven straight into a wall, such as Uber. (Pun intended.) In some cases, the companies started out fine, and made the decisions to take ethical shortcuts, usually because of a lethal combination of market forces and unethical staff (including leadership). In Twitter's case, we can almost pinpoint the exact second this happened: It's when they measured a Donald Trump tweet that broke their guidelines against the engagement it was getting, decided to leave it, and started defending that decision. In Facebook's case, the company is so big, there are both good and bad things going on inside. I'm sure that as the Death Star was destroying Alderaan, there were probably people falling in love on board. It still destroyed Alderaan. Those lovers still died when Luke made his trench run. The world is complicated. What I'm saying is that Facebook is as big as the Death Star. (Which, btw—inside job!)

Can those companies still be saved? Maybe, if they're suddenly overrun by people who want to work ethically, people who have a strong moral constitution, and people who are very, very patient. As I write this, Uber is under new leadership. That was an important first step. If Twitter did the same, there might be hope. Even then, there is nothing harder to change than company culture.

The bucket we haven't talked about yet is the truly odious. Ideas that are unethical to the core. Places where under no circumstances could you do good work, because doing work there and doing it to their definition of "well" would mean to do work that hurts others in some way. Yes, this is going to be one of those times where ethics and morals mix a bit, so strap in.

On March 17, 2017, the U.S. Department of Homeland Security published an RFP for a "Solid Concrete Border Wall" (Solicitation number HSBP1017R0022. You can look it up![24]) This is, of course, the idiotic wall Donald Trump proposed building along the U.S. and Mexican border to keep "Mexican rapists" (his words) out of the U.S. According to the Washington Post, Homeland Security received *hundreds* of submissions for that RFP. Which means at least *hundreds* of people sat down and came up with a plan to submit. I assume they were submitted by companies where multiple people worked, so conversations happened. Decisions were made. Designs were proposed. Feedback was given. Designs were revised. Obviously, I have no way of knowing this, but I wonder how many times, if any, the people doing this work turned to each other and said, "is a border wall a good idea?" What I do know is that, at least in those *hundreds* of companies, if someone did try to stop their company from replying to the RFP, it didn't work. They were submitted.

Some of the designs included a mall on the U.S. side of the wall. Many included amenities, as if the reason we believe concentration camps were awful was the lack of gift shops! These were cases of people attempting to "design away" the true horror of what they were creating. This was design as obfuscation. Not to mention a perversely concrete example of John Rawls' veil of ignorance—on one side of the wall you could shop, while on the other people died of hunger.

There is no way to ethically build a concrete border that separates families. We learned this in Berlin after defeating the Nazis the first time. (We will defeat them again.) You can't do your job well in a situation like that, because to do it well would mean hurting people. That's against the ethical code of design. There's no ethical way to design a gun because to design it well is to design it to kill better. We cannot do that.

Good work cannot be done in situations where the work is to hurt people, deceive them, or manipulate them.

Manipulate them? Holy shit, did I just throw the entire advertising industry under the bus? Yeah, I did. Well, hold off. Not entirely. If someone needs an oven and you convince them to buy yours instead of your competitor's without lying to them about what your oven is capable of doing, or what your competitor's is not capable of doing, by all means advertise it that way. That's enticement, not manipulation. If you tell them your oven does things it doesn't or can change their life in a way that's totally unrelated to the oven—This oven will get you laid!—that's manipulation, and you're being a dick. Don't be a dick.

Closer to home, you've got companies whose only goal is to deceive people. The clickbait farms. The fake news warehouses. The crackpot health companies like Theranos. The data miners. The genetics companies. The smart salt shaker startups. Stay away from those fools. You cannot do good work there.

DOES THE PERFECT PLACE TO WORK EXIST?

Of course not, but let me tell you a story.

A few weeks ago, I was having a conversation with my friend V (leaving her name out for obvious reasons.) She'd just gotten a new job. She was about a month in, which I realize is still within the honeymoon period. We'd had several conversations about her previous job in the past. Leadership was wishy-washy, coworkers were ultra-competitive, and she didn't always have the resources she needed to do her job. Yet, she's a good designer and she attempted to do good work there as long as she could.

"How's the new job?"

She replied that it was wonderful. Her face lit up. She said the leadership team was fantastic. They'd sat her down and explained where the company was going, and where it had made mistakes in the past, which made her trust them. She told me her coworkers were incredibly supportive. Everyone was united around a common goal. Yet, people weren't afraid to speak their piece when they felt something was wrong. Moreover, leadership listened to what they had to say. V felt respected within the company and she respected the people around her. She'd already been comfortable enough to put forth a few initiatives and got a positive response. This made her want to do her best work. I was happy for her.

Here's the important part: nothing that I just described is hard or expensive. Find a place with good leadership. Find a place that wants to listen to what you have to say. Find a place filled with people you want to collaborate with you, and people you're willing to collaborate with. If you're reading this and you run a company? Running that kind of place should be your goal. Like I said, it's not hard or expensive.

The people V works with aren't crushing code. They're not unicorns. They're working together to solve problems. That's a perfect place to work.

ETHICS AND PAYING RENT

Inevitably, when I bring up the topic of designers working ethically, someone will reply with some flavor of "that's nice, but I have rent to pay." Feel free to substitute "rent" for student loans, childcare, medical costs, and various other very real and very valid concerns. Along with what I'm guessing is a not-insignificant number of designers who are filling in that blank with "lifestyle to which I've grown accustomed."

Let's deal with the first group, since I have close to zero fucks to give for the second group. Either way, this promises to be less than enjoyable for both groups. It will neither give you permission to work unethically, nor outline a set of situations where working unethically is acceptable. If you think those reasons exist, you'd be wrong.

Where does this idea that you have to be open to tossing your ethics out the window to be successful come from? That's worth exploring a bit. Certainly, if we look around at the current landscape, we'll find plenty of examples of people who behaved—or continue to behave—unethically, and have done very well for themselves. From Travis Kalanick to Donald Trump, we see people who've broken the rules (pardon me—disrupted!), skirted regulation, and have generally behaved abominably towards others, to much success. In fact, it could be reasonably argued that in those particular cases, their success is due to their lack of ethics.

But if we look closely at those same individuals, we also see the price they've paid for their unethical success—the lack of trust, the constant vigilance, the scrutiny, and the eventual comeuppance. History won't remember these people kindly, and for that matter, the present isn't viewing them very kindly either.

Are they successful? Yes. For now. It's that little "for now" that you have to add that should give you pause. Their success is a house built on sand. Can you be successful by throwing ethics out the window? Yes, you can. You can also eat three burritos in one sitting. But in both situations, that act is coming back up on you, and it won't be pretty.

The fallacy of the road to success being paved by unethical work is just that, a fallacy. It's not a road. It's a dead end alley. It may provide a safe haven from the elements for a few minutes, but going from alley to alley to alley hoping you don't meet a dead end is a horrible way to complete a journey.

We've all been in spots where we've done things that were ethically questionable. We're human beings; we're messy. For example, I think we can all agree that stealing is wrong, yet none of us would hesitate to steal the proverbial loaf of bread to keep our families from starving. The problem comes when theft goes from being an emergency method to stave off starvation to the primary means through which you earn your income.

Throughout your career, you'll find yourself in spots where your only options might be doing a little work for one of the Travis Kalanicks of the world, or starving. By all means, don't starve! Just be honest with yourself about what you're doing, why you're doing it, and for how long you're going to do it. Because once you lose sight of that, the justifications start. ("I'm going to change things from the inside.") Realize that if you keep making those decisions, they end up defining your career. The idea that you can work unethically, build up a reputation, and then swing that ship around into ethical waters is also a fallacy. By that point, you do indeed have a reputation, but not the one you wanted. You'll find a bad reputation is the hardest thing in the world to change.

Think of it from the point of view of the person asking you to do the work. They're probably not totally unaware they're asking you to do some shady shit. They've probably convinced themselves it's a stop-gap. A temporary bit of shade to get the company back on track, perhaps. For example, I doubt Uber designed Greyball because they wanted to be evil. My guess is they imagined it was a necessarily small evil that helped them achieve a greater good. (You can justify anything if you try hard enough. Or just want to.) But in the end, everyone associated with that project is covered in shame, and their managers are probably looking at them like they were a shameful means to an end who they never want to see or think of again.

This is not the path to respect. It is not the path to a long career. This is a path to a career doing short stints of shame work.

I get it. You like to make things. You became a designer because you enjoyed designing. I did too, but there's more to this job than being happy someone is paying you to design something. We work within a tight, fragile ecosystem where our labor has repercussions. You are lucky enough to be a designer at a time when design is taken seriously and when design has power. With that power comes responsibility. You are responsible for what you put into the world. You are responsible for the effect your work has on the world. Right now, designers (I define this term broadly, as a reminder. Prick up your ears, developers and engineers!) are creating new inroads in all manner of things. We're designing software for self-driving cars. We're designing software which intimately touches people's lives. We're designing software which puts people in strangers' cars. We're designing databases which track immigrants for eventual deportation. All of these things need to be designed with the strictest ethics in mind. Some of these things don't pass an ethical test, and shouldn't be designed at all!

So, I get that you like making things, but making things at the expense of someone else's freedom is fucked. Deciding not to put what you're designing through an ethical test is not only lazy, it's dangerous. Feigning ignorance that ethics is not part of your job as a designer is no longer valid. Knowing that it's part of the job and ignoring it is criminal. Remember James Liang?

A better question than how you're going to pay your rent when working ethically might be why you are open to behaving unethically? Look around at the other professionals you interact with on a daily basis. Your doctor. Your grocer. Your mechanic. Your congressperson! How would you react to knowing they're entertaining doing their job unethically? Think of the ones who would appall you, and the ones you expect it from. Think about your relationship to the people on both those lists. I don't want designers on the same list as your congressperson. I'd be honored to be on the same list as your butcher.

How to Set Up for Success

Let's talk about Dr. Frances Oldham Kelsey.

She wasn't a designer. She was a pharmacologist and a physician. You've probably never heard of her. In fact, I found out about her from a Facebook group called "People who you should know but don't." They were correct on both counts. Dr. Kelsey was hired by the U.S. Food and Drug Administration in 1960. Her job was to review and test new drugs before they entered the U.S. market. I'm gonna go out on a limb here and say that in 1960, this was probably not an easy job for a woman to get, even for someone like Dr. Kelsey with a good reputation built on a successful career as a teacher at the University of Chicago and the University of South Dakota, and as a researcher. While researching a cure for malaria, Dr. Kelsey discovered that some drugs are able to pass through the placental barrier, which is important to our story.

She had the skills the FDA needed, so she went through what I imagine was a lengthy interview process. Met with a few people. They asked her questions. Some of them good, some of them no doubt irritating. Someone probably asked her who takes care of her children while she's at work. Maybe she did a couple of rounds of interviews. I'm sure they called references. Eventually, the FDA made the decision to hire Frances Oldham Kelsey. They hired her to do her job, which was to review and test new drugs before they hit the US market.

We are eternally glad they did so. I'll tell you why.

One of the first drugs assigned to her was thalidomide, a painkiller targeted at pregnant women for morning sickness. It had already been approved in twenty countries in Europe and Africa, as well as Canada. In other words, this should've been routine. Richardson Merrell, the pharmaceutical company that made thalidomide expected nothing less. All that needed to happen was for Frances Oldham Kelsey to give the green light.

Except that having been hired for a job, Dr. Frances Oldham Kelsey decided to do it. (I'll leave it up to you to decide if a male in her position would've done the job the same way.)

She went digging. She started doing research. She uncovered stories of women in those twenty countries who'd been prescribed thalidomide, and had subsequently gave birth to deformed infants. Deformities which were ultimately linked to thalidomide crossing the placental barrier, resulting in severe birth defects. By severe, I mean babies being born with no arms or legs. Richardson Merrell, despite putting a ton of pressure on her, never got their green light to release thalidomide in the United States, all because Dr. Frances Oldham Kelsey did her job. She stood at the gate and said this shall not pass. A job she kept doing for another forty-five years, by the way.

Although she was being paid by the FDA, and being pressured by a gigantic pharmaceutical company, she understood that her ultimate responsibility was to the women and children affected by that garbage drug. She had an ethical responsibility to do her job.

What does this have to do with design? Everything.

You were hired because someone decided you had a skill they needed. You probably went through a lengthy interview process. You met with a few people. They asked a bunch of questions, some of them good, some of them irritating. Hopefully, you asked some questions as well. Maybe they gave you a horrible design test, maybe they had you come back a couple of times, and then they made a decision to hire you. Numbers were

Dr. Frances Oldham Kelsey doing her job.

negotiated, papers were signed, and you were hired to be a profession-al designer. Congratulations. The people who hired you expect you to do your job, they also expect you to do it to the best of *your* ability, not to the best of theirs.

Like Dr. Kelsey, you were hired to do a job. You were hired for your judgment. You were hired to look out for the people affected by your work, no matter what pressure you might be getting to do otherwise. You were not hired to do someone's bidding. You were not hired to be some-one else's hands. You were not hired to green-light someone else's work without a second thought.

Even though someone may have hired you for your technical exper-tise, as is usually the case, the minute they hired a designer, they got the technical expertise *and* the ethical framework that goes with it. They cannot be separated. You do not need anyone's explicit permission to do your job the right way.

Frances Oldham Kelsey got her permission to do the job the right way the day she was hired. So did you.

I'm sure Frances Oldham Kelsey had some rough days at work for refusing to green-light thalidomide. With the benefit of hindsight, we know it was the right thing to do. Even though the expectation, especially for a drug that had already been approved in twenty other countries, was a quick green light. Keep things moving. Move onto the next drug to approve. Move fast and break things. Thankfully she didn't see it that way. She chose the path of being a pain-in-the-ass. Sometimes that's the job.

BE THE EXPERT

Here's what drives me nuts about designers, and please understand this is coming from a place of so much love. People hire you because you're an expert at what you do and your expertise is obviously needed or they wouldn't have hired a designer. Once you're through the door, you spend a lot of time asking the people who hired you how you should do your job. They told you they didn't know how to do your job when they hired you to do it!

Let's say your kitchen sink explodes. Most of us, me included, have no idea how to fix a busted sink. I know how to cut the water off, that's about it. So, after cutting the water off, I'm gonna call a plumber. I'm going to explain the situation, and they're gonna give me a quote. I'll tell them the quote is fine and then go watch TV while they fix the sink. If I'm lucky, I don't see the plumber again until the job is done. If I'm unlucky, they're in the living room every five minutes asking how I want something done, asking which tool they should use, asking if I mind they turn the water back on. Now, I get this isn't a perfect analogy, because good design is collaborative in nature, whereas fixing a sink feels like a solo job. But the point is that I've hired an expert and I expect they'll know how to do the job. I also expect that if they're trying to do the job while I'm hovering around them, they'll politely, but directly, tell me to back off and let them work.

People hire you to be the expert, so you might as well be the expert. Tell those people what it's going to take to do your job and how you're going to do it. And if you're walking into a situation where you're supposed to fit into a certain methodology of working, get clarity on what that methodology is and whether you're okay with it *before* you accept the job.

Designers are not simply cogs in their machines. We're the oil that makes it all work.

THE MYTH OF APPROVAL

You were also not hired to get someone's approval.

Let me tell you another story about that presenting workshop I do. I've had engineers, developers, product managers, etc., in the workshop, but by and large, it's career designers. Part of the workshop includes every participant giving a five-minute presentation. Before launching into their presentation, each participant needs to set the stage by telling us the goal of the presentation. Almost every designer goes up there and says their goal is to "get approval" for their work, as if they're being graded. As if they're presenting their work to their parents with the hope they'll stick the work on the company fridge.

You were not hired to get approval or to be graded or to have your work pinned to the company fridge. Too often, designers present their work as if the goal is to get someone to like it, as if our job is to make someone happy. (Ask yourself how many times you've ended a presentation with "Do you like it?") That's not the job. You were hired to solve problems. Your work should be evaluated on how well it solves those problems (without creating new ones.)

The minute you start saying things like, "I'm here for your approval," all of that goes out the window. The very first thing we need to do to set ourselves up for success, and to be able to do the job we were hired for, is to remove subjective and reductive language from our vocabulary. Part of the problem here is the myth of imposter syndrome.

Let's put imposter syndrome to bed once and for all. If you got hired after going through a lengthy interview process where you interviewed multiple times with multiple people, there's really only two options. One—everyone who interviewed you is an idiot and you somehow managed to pull one over on them. That's actually pretty unlikely. You might've been able to fool one or two, but not the whole lot. Or two—you're actually as good as the people who interviewed you thought you were. That seems like the more reasonable option, so stop it with the imposter syndrome stuff.

When someone decides you've earned the right to call yourself a professional designer and get paid for it—believe them. You only need to get hired for a job once. After that, you get to do it. No, you have to do it.

WHO DO YOU WORK FOR, AGAIN?

Remember earlier in the book when I told you that you didn't work for the people who wrote your checks? That's worth going into again here, keeping our new friend Dr. Frances Oldham Kelsey in mind. I guarantee you, her decision to do further research on thalidomide caused headaches at the FDA—and to be fair, her supervisors stood by her the entire time. I'm betting that pharmaceutical company was breathing down the FDA's neck to get this thing done. Pharmaceutical companies tend to be pricks about this shit. She would've made their lives a lot easier by just going ahead and green-lighting this thing. No one would've blamed her. Twenty countries had already done the same. But she remembered who she worked for. Wasn't the FDA. Sure as shit wasn't the pharmaceutical company. She worked for the women who'd be prescribed this drug. You work for the people who'll ultimately come in contact with your work. You work for the people who aren't in the room. Sadly, that also means they aren't in the room to back you up, or to urge you on, or to give you the courage you need to stand up for them, or to thank you for having done it.

The people who can make you uncomfortable are in the room, and that can be intimidating. I totally get that.

There will be times you're asked to do things that run counter to the best interests of the people you work for. You cannot do it.

There will be times you're not sure whether the things you're being asked to do will be in their best interests or not. In fact, that's gonna happen fairly often. That's when you need to buckle down and buy time to find out for sure. You work the case. You do the research. You talk to the people you work for. You ask questions. You work the use cases. That's the job. That's the job you signed up for. Don't ask for permission to do your job. You got it when they hired you, although you may have to remind the people who pay you once in a while.

THE MYTH OF THE SOLITARY GENIUS

Silicon Valley loves the myth of the solitary genius. Solitary *boy* genius to be exact. Solitary *white* boy genius, if we really want to get down to it. So does Hollywood. In fact, we were lucky enough to have the myth explained to us in *The Social Network*. The maybe-it's-true, maybe-it's-not story of the invention of Facebook. In the movie, the solitary boy genius, Mark Zuckerberg gets scorned by a woman (every wallet in Silicon Valley just opened) and uses that as the impetus for creating a social network to rank the bangability of other college women. (The part where Facebook started as an app to do *just that* is true, by the way.) He works to the wee hours in his dorm room. He doesn't eat. He doesn't bathe. He musses his hair! He writes on the windows. On windows! This is how we're sold the idea of his genius. He is driven in his quest to create a thing that only he can create and only by being free of women can he create it! So genius. Much brooding. So close to human.

So destructive.

This idiotic myth runs rampant through the industry. Work is created by solitary brooding young men on their dorm room windows, on the back of paper napkins while sitting in children's playgrounds, on the way to and from Burning Man, and while sitting in hot tubs with VCs wondering if they're supposed to pull their swimsuit off too. Sadly, like a dog that's continuously surprised by its own farts, Silicon Valley has told this story so many times, it's started believing it. While it may be true that the very bare germ of an idea might in fact come from a single person—who may even be a woman or person of color!—those very bare germs need the help of a lot more people before they can become anything that's even remotely qualified to be called an idea, much less a good idea.

Why is this myth so resonant with our industry? That's a really good question, right? Why is it so important to believe that ideas spring fully formed from the mind of a solitary genius? I mean, our mythology is sloppy with it. From the seven labors of Hercules, to Beowulf, to Sisyphus, to Paul Bunyon, to Thor crushing code and dark elves with his mighty hammer, to John Galt single-handedly rebuilding capitalism in *Atlas Shrugged*. We love our brooding solitary boy heroes. All of Silicon Valley is a revenge fantasy about getting picked last at dodgeball.

Venture capitalists have a thing they like to say. "We don't invest in ideas. We invest in people." That's true in a couple of ways. Let's get the funny one out of the way: they don't invest in ideas. Check. They invest in people. Specifically, they invest in people who look like they do, because today's venture capitalist was yesterday's startup founder and vice versa. They might as well be saying "we're both investing in our younger selves, and reinvesting in the idea that we've earned our place by perpetuating the idea that the next wave of us will come from the same pool."

The more we invest in the myth of the brooding solitary boy genius, the more we can retroactively claim that mantle as our own. Genius recognizes genius, right? Imagine being so insecure that you spend your life justifying your own career by uplifting people who look like you to reinforce the idea that you come from genius stock.

Y Combinator's Paul Graham, one of Silicon Valley's most powerful men, once told the New York Times[25]:

"I can be tricked by anyone who looks like Mark Zuckerberg. There was a guy once who we funded who was terrible. I said: 'How could he be bad? He looks like Zuckerberg!'"

THE IMPORTANCE OF DIVERSE TEAMS

From the get-go, Mule was fifty percent female. Easy to do when there are two of you and one is female. As we've grown, we've tried very consciously to maintain a good balance. Never, not once, have we not hired the best person for the job. We've never decided ahead of time that we needed to hire a woman or a man for a particular role. What we've done is make sure that everyone had an equal opportunity to be hired. Lo and behold, we've found that when you give a population that's roughly fifty percent female an equal chance, you end up with a roughly fifty percent female staff. The point isn't to aim for a certain percentage though. The point is to foster an environment where different viewpoints are not just welcomed, but encouraged. When women apply here, they see themselves reflected in who's interviewing them, making this feel like a more welcoming place.

Why is this important? Because we're trying to design great products. We've found that the more diverse points-of-view we let into the design process, the better our work is, the more likely it is to be understood by a broader segment of the population, and the more successful our clients are because of it. We already have one person who thinks like me in the office. (It's enough). We want to create an environment with as many different experiences, viewpoints, and ways of looking at the world and solving problems as possible. We've found that getting the opinions and insights of people with a variety of experiences to be critical in doing good work. Because society defines gender roles along very similar paths—I'm painting with a very broad brush here—the best way to get a woman's viewpoint is from a woman herself! Yes, I realize they come in various shapes, sizes, experiences, and flavors, but I can guarantee that none of those mirror mine. With a little bit of research, empathy, and acting I may be able to almost-kinda-sorta see things from the point of view of a guy who likes cars, golf, and nachos; but no amount of empathy or research will ever, ever allow me to design things from a woman's point-of-view. Just like I will never be able to experience the world from a Black person's point of view.

So, what's the problem? Easy. We don't have enough women! Although women account for more than fifty percent of the general population, they account for quite a bit less than that in the design workforce and as you head up the chain, whether in positions of leadership or influence, that percentage shrinks dramatically. To the point where it's not uncommon to attend a design conference with absolutely no women on stage. When you don't see yourself reflected in those positions of authority, you begin believing they aren't accessible to you.

What about merit? Great question, if it weren't that the merit argument is used in the most ironic way possible. I'd ask why a small percentage of the population (for the sake of argument, let's use white males as our example) has merited taking such a high percentage of available opportunities? Could it be that they are inherently more qualified than other groups? Of course not. No one would argue that point, lest they be thought a fool. That would be akin to arguing that Jackie Robinson was the first Black ballplayer good enough for the major leagues. One could argue that those white males are better known, and they'd be right. This has less to do with merit than with a systematic underrepresentation of women and minorities.

As designers, we are tasked with solving the problems of the world. The more we and those we look up to reflect the face of the world around us, the better our solutions will be. If we continue to behave like it's a white man's world, we're not only doing ourselves a disservice, we're doing our society a disservice.

Isn't this a quota? So what? I take no small amount of delight in people who start screaming for fairness only once what they've denied others is being taken from them. I don't have an issue with a bit of over-correcting if need be. We've been erring on the other side for a bit, it seems fair to err on this one for a bit.

Sometimes merit needs a push. You can't level a playing field without bringing in a few bulldozers.

The first step of setting up for success is including as many different points of view in the room from as many different cultures as possible with as many experiences as possible. The fact that Chuck went to Berkeley while Todd and Stew went to Stanford is not diversity.

SETTING THE RIGHT GOALS

Why are you building what you're building? What problem is it fixing? Who, besides the people in charge, stand to benefit from your labor?

The first question we ask anyone we're in the process of engaging with at Mule is "why are you making this?" If the answer comes back as any version of "because there's an opportunity to make money," we're out.

Obviously, making money is important in most endeavors. When it's the primary reason for doing something, I begin to worry. First of all, money-making opportunities change with the wind. You don't want to get into a months—or years—long relationship with someone based on where the wind is currently blowing. Secondly, and most importantly, when people's main driver is financial, that means the health of the people using the product and the products effects on society are by definition secondary.

Let's make the point using our favorite punching bag, Twitter. Twitter's main goal is to make money. In their quest for money, they've allowed their platform to be overrun by Nazis, white supremacists, and other agents of harassment and abuse, because those people drive engagement. Twitter makes money from engagement. When I say that Twitter hasn't done anything about abuse on their platform I'm not being totally honest—they've profited from it.

On September 23, 2017, Donald Trump tweeted out a direct threat to North Korea. (For the record, North Korea replied that they saw it as a declaration of war.[26] The bluster was on both sides.) Within minutes of Trump's tweet, Twitter sent me an email with the tweet, in case I'd missed

Donald J. Trump ✔
@realDonaldTrump

Follow

Just heard Foreign Minister of North Korea speak at U.N. If he echoes thoughts of Little Rocket Man, they won't be around much longer!

8:08 PM - 23 Sep 2017

32,899 Retweets **123,881** Favorites

💬 47K 🔁 33K ⭐ 124K ✉️

it, in case my heart wasn't racing fast enough. Because their main goal is making money. At any expense.

Making money is a requirement of starting and maintaining a business, but it's not a goal.

Over the years we've worked with some amazing clients with a variety of goals, and yes, all of them needed to make money. They were all able to answer the question of "why are you making this?" with some version of "because it helps people." Whether it was to help people do something incredibly important like access their healthcare records or something silly like find gifs of baby goats—don't underestimate the mental health benefits of baby goat gifs!—everything your labor is used for should have the goal of helping people. While that may sound a little high-minded, it's really not. Using our labor to help others should be the basic minimum that we aspire to.

KNOW WHERE THE MONEY COMES FROM

Fans of *The Wire* will be familiar with Lester Freamon's important lesson: "Follow the money." Always know where the money is coming from, how the money gets made, and where the money is going.

Since you're probably working somewhere that relies on money to stay afloat, it's in your best interest to know as much about that money in order to design solutions, as well as to make sure the money is coming from and being used in ways you can ethically stand behind. Let's look at some common business cases:

Slack, for example, makes money by selling subscriptions to their enterprise software. The more people use it, the more money they make. Your company wants to use Slack, they pay. They keep using it, they keep paying. If they make more money from subscriptions than they spend, they make money. Easy peasy. Makes sense and is easy enough to follow.

The New York Times and many other newspapers use a combination of advertising and a subscription paywall. Meaning that until you ante up for a subscription, they limit the amount of articles you can read.

Twitter makes money by getting you to fight with Nazis.

Facebook is a fun case. They make money a thousand different ways. Advertising, sure, but you can also pay them to insert content into the newsfeed. This is where things begin to get fishy. As we saw from the "fake news" crisis of the 2016 election, Facebook either did a shitty job of tracking who was paying for inserting these stories, or they knew and didn't care. When called before Congress, Facebook ended up releasing over three thousand examples of "ads" containing false information bought before the 2016 election, many of them paid for with rubles. Like Lester said, "follow the money." I imagine it's fairly easy to track where an ad buy is coming from, if you want to. After all, they weren't going out of their way to hide it.

Facebook also makes money by selling our data, which we keep giving them. On August 17, 2018, the Washington Post reported that Facebook was about to get serious about asking you to give them your banking data, so you can check account balances and such right on the platform. This was shortly after the Cambridge Analytica hack where almost 100,000 users' data was gobbled up by a data firm working on the Trump election campaign.

All of these monetization systems are designed and built by people like us. Sometimes we know what they're for and don't care. Sometimes we don't know what they're for and don't ask. Both are just as bad.

If you care about working ethically, it is imperative that you understand how your company makes money, because your labor is going to be used to help them do it. The second question we ask all of our clients after "why are you making this?" is "how does this make money?"

Turns out that helping them answer that question is an important design problem as well. If you don't have a clear answer from the get go, you'll eventually find yourself in a dilemma where you're short on cash and looking around for what's valuable. That answer is usually what your users' hold most dear: their private information. I don't care what it says in your terms of service, that's some unethical shady shit.

THE IMPORTANCE OF RESEARCH

Very early on in our company's life, we decided we could no longer work with early-stage startups, even if they had a good reason for what they were building, and could answer the money question. The reasons may relate back to the solitary genius issue. We were getting calls from people who had a fully formed idea in their head, and they were looking for someone to take that idea, which was already real to them, and make it real for others.

Mule is a research-based design shop. We're firm believers that solving a problem can't happen until you understand the problem. That generally means talking to the people who are having the problem. Once we understand it, we'll come up with a few solutions, then evaluate them based on whether the people having the problem can use the thing we made to make the problem go away. (For more on research, check out Erika Hall's *Just Enough Research*. She explains it better than I do.)

We were finding that early-stage startups (again, I'm generalizing a bit) weren't interested in doing research. They just wanted the thing in their head made real. They wanted us to execute their vision. In my experience, fear of doing research is always about ego and fear, which is a horrible combination. If you have a good idea, you should be *happy* that someone is willing to kick the tires on it. You should be demanding it, actually. You want to know if your idea will actually work. Believing you have a great idea is good, knowing your idea is great is even better. If you're afraid of having those tires kicked, it's because you know there's something wrong or you're afraid there's something wrong. So, beware of someone who doesn't want you to look behind the curtain, kick the tires, and have their assumptions tested. All of those things are part of your job. Helping people realize shitty ideas in order to preserve their ego is an equally shitty way to earn a living.

GATHERING THE RIGHT FEEDBACK

Try as you might, there is no guarantee the work you put into the world won't be misused. None. In fact, you should assume your work gets misused the minute it goes live. It's what people do. There are, however, steps you can take while making something to minimize misuse. There are also steps you need to take during the lifecycle of your product or service to keep it healthy.

It's human nature to look for faults in other people's work, which is something we can use to our advantage by having people find those faults before the work goes live. Tire kicking is a gift. If someone kicks the tires on your work and it falls apart, that person is your new best friend because they just saved your ass. They helped you keep bad work out of the world.

The goal of feedback isn't to find out if people like what you made. We already discussed that. "I like it" isn't good feedback. It's shitty feedback.

It contains exactly zero information. "This right here is broken" is good feedback. It tells you there is a problem. You can explore that further. Ask the person how it's broken. Keep digging until you get to the root of what the problem is, and then fix it.

I've written about getting and giving good feedback in my previous two books, *Design Is a Job* and *You're My Favorite Client*. You should read those. They're filled with good foundation stuff for starting a design career and for working with clients. For the purposes of this book, I want to stay with the role of feedback and ethics. It is absolutely wrong to release something into the world that you know has a problem. That means you need to gather people together to elicit their feedback on what you've made and you should hand them sledgehammers with a smile on your face.

THE GARDEN METAPHOR YOU'VE BEEN WAITING FOR

Nothing you make is ever truly done. In fact, the story of your work starts when it passes from your hands and into the world. Because all the good work that you did to ensure the work is good, and that its impact is beneficial, can only truly be evaluated when it's finally out in the world.

Anyone who's ever started a garden knows that the real work starts the day you plant it. For those of you trying to keep up with the metaphor, that would be the day you release your product out into the world. You need to water. You need to weed. You need to check on the health of what's growing. You've got to support your tomatoes as they grow taller. Then the vermin show up. From the viral, to the bacterial, to the cloven-hoofed, everything wants to eat from your garden. With each new menace, you have to protect what you're growing.

Because you started your garden with the goal of feeding your family healthy food, you can't just go after the vermin with pesticides. That puts your goal at risk as much as allowing the vermin to run free. Ultimately, you want your garden to be a place where your fruits and vegetables thrive, and that takes work.

Success isn't just launching. That's the easy part! You could plow a couple of square feet of dirt in your backyard tomorrow and throw seeds at it. There's your minimal-viable-product garden! But by morning, you'd have happy squirrels and no seeds. Today's solitary genius gardener would then proceed to build a squirrel proof garden, only to find out about moles a couple of nights after that, and so forth.

Instead, you could do a little research about the pests in your area, and how to proof the garden against them. You can also take a walk around the neighborhood, meet the neighbors, see who else has a garden. What failures and successes have they had? (They'll tell you. People with gardens love talking about their gardens.) Are you the only one who cooks in your house? Gather up everyone who does and see what they'd like to plant. They can also help ensure a healthy garden.

Then after you've planted everything together, you begin the real work, ensuring that everything grows. You're gonna have to pull weeds. You're gonna have to build supports. You're gonna have to keep an eye out for disease and vermin. Gardens, like every other thing we bring into the world, need to be tended. There are things we want in it and things we don't. Every year that we plant, we learn. If we're having terrible luck with snap peas, we might decide to stop planting snap peas, and dedicate that patch of dirt to growing tomatoes instead.

A mole that sneaks into your garden will eventually eat everything you planted, leaving your family hungry. That mole is not ensuring your success. Worst yet, it's gonna go back to mole town and tell the other moles there's a really easy garden to get into. Then you got a real mole problem. (You get I'm talking about Twitter and Nazis here, right? Good.) You need to ban that mole from your garden. You need to send the other moles a message.

You cannot find a mole in your garden and decide the mole is engagement. Unless, of course, engaging with moles was your goal all along, in which case I question your decisions.

The work we do lives in the world. We make it. It affects the people who come in contact with it. It's our solemn duty to make sure it's well thought out, beneficial, and as free from error as possible once it's in their hands. Even then, we owe them vigilance.

Ultimately, the success we crave isn't our own. It's the success of the people we work for. The ones on the ground. We want the work we do to be successful for them. That's the job.

Oh, The Monsters We'll Kill

On April 21, 2018, an eighteen-year-old woman went to her senior prom in Salt Lake City, Utah.

I'm purposely not using her name for reasons that I hope will become evident. This story has both ordinary bits and extraordinary bits. I'll start with the ordinary bits. She was white, which, if you know anything about Salt Lake City, you'll agree is ordinary. She was wearing a dress she picked out at her local thrift store. Like ninety-nine percent of the people going to their high school proms, she posted photos of herself and her friends to social media, which is what we built social media for them to do. Again, ordinary.

Here's another ordinary thing she did, although I have a feeling some of you may disagree with me. The dress she bought at that thrift store and was wearing in those prom photos was a traditional Chinese qipao dress. Cultural appropriation? You bet. Bad taste? Without a doubt. So, why am I putting it in the ordinary column? Because eighteen-year-olds do stupid things. They've been doing stupid things since the beginning of time. I did *amazingly* stupid things at that age and so did you. In fact, some people, me included, would say that doing stupid things, especially at the age of eighteen, is an integral part of learning. We do dumb shit. The people around us tell us it's dumb, maybe shame us a little, avoid us for a little bit and we, hopefully, learn not to repeat that mistake.

So why are we talking about this at all, if it's so ordinary? Because what happened next was anything but ordinary. The photos of this eighteen-year-old and her dress, which she posted, went viral. People had opinions on it—as people are wont to have. Articles were written. Eventually, someone made a Twitter Moment out of the whole thing. The icing on the cake: Twitter started promoting that moment. That last bit right there is what makes this story extraordinary. A publicly traded corporation was driving engagement of, and profiting off, the cyberbullying of an eighteen-year-old who'd done a dumb thing. Twitter, a company where designers work and make decisions, was making money from publicly shaming an eighteen-year-old who did a dumb thing. It was doing it because it was designed to work that way.

Hopefully, we can agree on this: as dumb and thoughtless as her cultural appropriation was, no eighteen year old deserves the weight of the internet on their head for making a dumb decision. It's beyond a measured response. If you've ever caught yourself thinking you were glad the internet wasn't around when you were eighteen, you should think about what it's doing to the kids for whom it's ubiquitous.

Hopefully, we can also agree on this: we shouldn't be designing platforms that enable, much less promote or profit from, bullying.

Living online is still a fairly new phenomenon. I still vividly remember the day I got my first computer, the day I installed my first AOL disc, then the day AOL added a "World Wide Web" link (complete with a spider web graphic), and then the day I downloaded Mosaic. I remember the first day I "friended" someone, which was quickly followed by "unfriending" someone and, of course, the eventual blocking. Like many designers of my generation, I was trained to design things in a world before all of those things were possible. I was taught form, typography, aesthetics, color theory, etc. By the time the phrase "UX" was invented, I'd already been doing it for a while. I learned by the seat of my pants, like many of the people my age. We were neither trained, nor did we grow up with it. In some cases, we bear the responsibility of inventing the things you're interacting with online or speaking to in your kitchen, but that doesn't mean we understand how they affect people.

To be quite honest, we're using young people—who have never known a life without these platforms—as lab rats in our unethical experiments.

Let's talk about depression.

Like about twenty percent of the world, I have to deal with it. (I'm lucky enough to have access to care when I need it.) One of my warning signs is when I can't tell the difference between a big problem and a small problem. My brain stops prioritizing. Every problem comes at me as exactly the same size. This is depression taking away a major coping mechanism. That's exactly how we've designed Twitter. Every outrage is the exact same size, whether it was a US president declaring war on a foreign nation or a movie we remember fondly from our childhood being recast with (gasp!) women in the lead roles or an eighteen-year-old who made a stupid decision on what to wear to the prom. On Twitter, those problems become exactly the same size. They receive the same amount of outrage. They're presented identically. They're just as big as one another. Twitter works like a giant depressed brain. It can't tell right from wrong, and it can't tell big from small. It needs help.

The thing is, my brain works that way because it's broken, so I get it treatment. Twitter works that way by design. Twitter is working exactly like Twitter's leadership team wants it to be working. The constant outrage, the hatred, the anxiety, the harassment—it's all by design. It's engagement, and engagement brings them money and raises their stock price. They have no interest in changing it. If they wanted to do so, they would've taken real steps to change it.

Twitter's never taken a step against harassment. They've taken steps to stop bad public relations. That is very different. They care about their brand, not the people using their service. You might think that's a cynical viewpoint, but when Donald Trump tweets about nuclear war with North Korea, Twitter packages it into an email blast to make sure you see it. They are monetizing that moment of panic.

I believe Twitter has a social responsibility to help make the world a better place. All companies do. We need to challenge the idea that a CEO's primary mission is to make money for shareholders. That may be one of their missions, but to single that out as a primary mission is irresponsible. Society simply can't afford for your business to make money without regard to the impact it has on the environment. We learned this when McDonald's cleared the Amazon rainforest to grow soy to feed factory chickens and cattle[27]. Society simply can't afford for your business to make money without regard to the impact it has on your clients' physical well-being. We learned this when Philip Morris was knowingly blowing cancer in our lungs. Society simply can't afford for your business to make money without regard to the impact it has on our mental well-being. We're learning this now as Jack Dorsey lines the bank accounts of his shareholders with the fruits of our anxiety.

Twitter has purposefully, knowingly used anxiety and fear to build a business. Sadly, they're not alone. We're at the edge of the map. We're in "here there be dragons" territory. We're designing things the long term affects of which we have little understanding. Or none. In part, it's because we're designing things we haven't been trained to design. Today's platforms require an understanding of skills we were never taught. We might have better luck teaching psychologists how to design for the web instead of teaching UX designers how to learn the psychological tools we need for this new landscape. We're strip-mining humanity for engagement and fracking the decency out of society because we're working within a system of rewards that doesn't give a damn about long-term effects, only short-term gains. Silicon Valley doesn't care what the long-term effects of an eighteen-year-old being bullied on Twitter is as long as they're discovered after the options vest and the stock is sold.

Hopefully, I've convinced you by now that your job is to be a line of defense against monsters. Because it's time to meet some of the monsters at the gate.

DECEPTIVE PATTERNS

Deceptive patterns are the low-hanging fruit of design ethics. They're generally easy to spot. They keep people from doing what they intended to do. They rob users of their intent, because their intent runs counter to how a business makes their money. Your job is to make it easy for people to do what they want. Deceptive patterns are designed to do just the opposite. Imagine you're driving on a toll road, and the sign for your exit ends up routing you back onto the toll road, or is hidden behind a tree, or moves from place to place as you try to read it, or is printed blue on blue to match the sky. That's a deceptive pattern. It makes the thing you're trying to do harder instead of easier. Deceptive patterns are the canaries in the coal mine of unethical design. A company who's willing to keep a customer hostage is willing to do worse.

Also, we're not talking about things like "are you *sure* you want to delete all your photos?" That's a failsafe. We're talking about hiding the link that says "yes, I am sure."

Deceptive patterns are Level 1 shit. That's the level of the video game where you learn how the character moves, how far you can jump, and how the world is laid out. If you can't succeed at this level, you don't get to go to Level 2. They happen at the interface level, for which designers are directly responsible. Even designers just starting out will have to fight the deceptive pattern fight. Think of them as the goombas in Mario games: easy to kill, but pervasive and annoying as fuck.

You cannot take someone's intent away. There are no ethical reasons to design deceptive patterns, no matter what Brad from Marketing tells you. Brad is a liar.

MANIPULATIVE LANGUAGE

On the one hand, manipulative language is messed up. On the other hand, I'm glad there's an internet job my mom is qualified for. I'm talking about the language on buttons and links used to talk you out of doing the thing you want to do. In the section above, we talked about making the users' intent hard to accomplish through obfuscation. Another way of stealing intent is to keep the choice out in the open, but be incredibly manipulative with the language you're using.

"No thanks, I don't want to get smarter."

"I have enough friends and I enjoy being lonely."

"I enjoy being fat, thanks."

"Yes, I *do* want to die alone."

This is nothing but passive aggressive shaming. Would you want someone talking to you like that? No, you would not. Then don't talk to anyone else that way. Use clear language that communicates what's going on. Be upfront about what things do and what effects they'll have. "We're sorry to see you go" is fine, "if you leave, we're going to be totally depressed and it'll be your fault" is not.

Oh, but Mike, I don't write the words. C'mon. You know that excuse isn't gonna fly. We're too far along. Whether you're writing them or not, you're a checkpoint. They're coming through *your* gate. You cannot let them. Also, offer to write them. Designers should be able to write their own interface language.

ADDICTIVE SOFTWARE

On March 13, 2017, Adam Alter, the author of *Irresistible: The Rise of Addictive Technology and the Business of Keeping Us Hooked*, went on NPR's *Fresh Air* to talk about addictive software. He made a frightening observation:

> *Ten years ago, before the iPad and iPhone were mainstream, the average person had an attention span of about twelve seconds. Now research suggests that there's been a drop from twelve to eight seconds... shorter than the attention of the average goldfish, which is nine seconds.*

We've made people more scatterbrained than goldfish. Alter goes on to describe scans that show how our brain patterns as we fire up apps, games, and social media sites match up almost perfectly with brain scans of addicts looking for their next hit.

On January 23, 2019, Elle Hunt published an extensive piece in The Guardian[28] about a new condition being referred to as "Snapchat dysmorphia." People want to match what they look like in their filtered images. They worry about meeting an online friend in person because they won't match the images they've been putting out. The filters we're designing to make our online photos look "good" are making us hate how we look, and we're looking to surgery to correct it. Unsurprisingly, it's hitting adolescents the hardest. The kids are going through enough.

On September 17, 2018, the New Yorker published a devastating profile on Mark Zuckerberg, written by Evan Osnos, titled *Can Mark Zuckerberg Fix Facebook Before It Breaks Democracy*[29]. I encourage you to find and read the whole thing, but let me point out this particular passage:

> At an event in November, 2017, Sean Parker, Facebook's first president, called himself a "conscientious objector" to social media, saying, "God only knows what it's doing to our children's brains." A few days later, Chamath Palihapitiya, the former vice-president of user growth, told an audience at Stanford, "The short-term, dopamine-driven feedback loops that we have created are destroying how society works—no civil discourse, no coöperation, misinformation, mistruth." Palihapitiya, a prominent Silicon Valley figure who worked at Facebook from 2007 to 2011, said, "I feel tremendous guilt. I think we all knew in the back of our minds." Of his children, he added, "They're not allowed to use this shit."

The sentence I want you to focus on there is "I think we all knew in the back of our minds." There are a million articles, think pieces, and hot takes on what social media is doing to our kids. Very few of them ask the question "who built this shit?" We built it. We lined our pockets with the profits—and then we question the motivation and the drive of the generations that got addicted to the drugs we manufactured for them. It's telling that Chamath Palihapitiya won't let his kids use "this shit" he had a hand in building. I'm curious about a couple of things: will he be returning the profit he made from addicting other people's kids? And what's he doing to stop it from happening?

DATA COLLECTION MALPRACTICES, OVER

There's one design test I give interviewees at Mule. (I stole it from legendary designer Kim Goodwin, who's smarter than I am. By the way, I never told her I stole her design test. She'll only ever find out if she reads this book. Ethics!) I write a bunch of form labels on the whiteboard, in a nonsensical order, along with a bunch of randomly sized input boxes. I include first name, last name, address, gender, city, state, email address, etc. Then I tell the interviewee that we're designing a form to sign up for an email newsletter and to arrange them in the right order. Only people who ask me why I need the users' gender, or physical address, or really, anything but their email address get a second interview. I won't hire a designer who doesn't ask why, and I won't hire a designer whose desire to arrange boxes is more important than their desire to protect users' data.

The data we collect from users should be the absolute bare minimum in order to do the thing we are telling them is happening. The thing we are telling them is happening needs to be what's *actually* happening. If you want more of their data to do something else later, you need to tell the user. If you, as the designer, don't know what that something else is, do not let it make it onto the interface.

We already have enough data that's going to take us hundreds of years to process. That's if we decided what we wanted to do with it *today*. We do not know what we want to do with it. We've just collected it. Tell Brad he can collect new data once he's analyzed the data he already has.

Of course, the reason companies collect the data is that when everything else fails, they can sell that data to someone else. (No, that company won't know what to do with it, either.) People who know what to do with data also know how to steal it, so they don't bother to buy it. We know all too well that data breaches aren't rare. By mid 2018, according to the Identity Theft Resource Center (ITRC), we had already surpassed the number of breached records for the entirety of 2017. That includes 5 million records at Lord & Taylor, over 19 million records at the Sacramento Bee, 27 million records at Ticketfly, 37 million records at Panera Bread (Seriously? Who the fuck is giving Panera Bread their data?), 92 million records at MyHeritage, 150 million records at UnderArmour, and of course close to 100 million records at Facebook, via their esteemed partner Cambridge Analytica. I'm gonna guess Facebook might've had more of your data than Panera Bread. An industry that can't keep your data safe cannot have more of it. (Two weeks after I wrote that sentence, Facebook had another breach of 50 million accounts. There's no way to write this and keep the numbers current.)

So, no. You cannot collect lots of extra data just in case.

DATA COLLECTION MALPRACTICES, UNDER

At the same time that we collect too much data, we still manage to display a great deal of willful ignorance with the data choices that we do give people. If you absolutely *must* ask for someone's gender, the choices must be more inclusive than male and female. (Again, ask yourself *why* you need to know this to begin with. What are you going to *do* with it? That answer may expose an even greater problem, such as a decision to target market pink or blue baby clothes.) If you honestly have a real reason that you need to know someone's gender, just leave it an open field. People are gloriously complex. As a designer, I'm not going to trade someone's happiness for a dataset that's easier to sort.

Let's talk about names. Names are probably easier. On November 9, 2017, Twitter did a good thing. (Insert stopped clock metaphor.) They increased the character count of their name field from twenty characters to fifty. Their reasoning for this is there are places and cultures where people have much longer names than in the US, where Twitter was born. (Of course it took them over ten years to realize this.) If you're designing for a global audience, you need to design not *for*, but *with*, that global audience. For the record, all the Twitter founders' names fit within the original twenty character limit. Had there been someone on that team from a culture that tends to go long on names, chances are they would've rolled out of the gate with a longer name limit.

At least names are easier than gender. Oh, wait. Except for when they're tied to it. OKCupid still insists trans people use their "legal" or dead name on their accounts. This puts an undue burden on people who can't or choose not to (their reasons are not your business) legally change their name, meaning they have to either go by their dead name, break the terms of service, or not use the service. Policies like this can also out people in vulnerable positions, or in less-than-friendly locations with horrible repercussions including losing their jobs and physical violence. This is discrimination by legality.

So no, asking people for their names is not an easy question. Your name is your identity. Identity is a choice.

Maybe race will be easier to discuss than names. I almost couldn't finish that sentence! Look, if you're going to ask people for their race, ask yourself what the worst people in the world would do with that information. Such as landlords on AirBnB refusing to rent to people based on race. (Happened.) Or political campaigns using racial profiling to target specific racist ads to people of specific races. (Also happened.) So again, when someone tells you to design something to collect a specific piece of data, ask them what they intend to do with that data. You have a right to know, after all, the work they're asking you to do is going out with your name on it. Plus, you may be able to design a way that gets them what they need while also protecting the person interacting with the tool you built.

STALKING-MADE-EASY

In May of 2018, Tinder started beta testing a new feature in Australia and Chile. They call it Places[30]. Places keeps track of every place you've been in through your phone's GPS (and via a partnership with Foursquare). If you go to the gym, it'll tell you which of the other people there might be potential matches for you. Coffeehouse two doors down? Same thing. Wanna follow a potential hook-up to the grocery store? Places makes it easy to follow someone along a daily path. The other word for this is stalking.

Previously, Tinder also added people's place of employment to their profiles.

In 2016, Uber announced that it would be tracking its riders for a full five minutes after they got out of vehicles, regardless of whether you were still using the app or not. According to them, they were tracking how many of their riders had to cross the street after a drop-off. The tracking was for safety reasons. Perhaps that was the intent. But the end result is a tool for stalking people.

In 2014, a popular San Francisco coffee shop, Philz, started using a service named Euclid to track customer movements[31]. Euclid would grab your phone's MAC address when you walked in the store and then track where you stood, which direction you went when you walked out, and how often you came back. They stopped shortly after customers got skeeved out by it.

Digital surveillance is easy and a lot of people are still so excited that they *can* do it, they haven't begun worrying about whether they *should* do it. Now that everyone carries GPS devices in their pockets, it's possible to know where they are all the time. Users themselves are still pretty excited at the idea that the world knows where they are at all times. They're willing to exchange that information for a fifteen percent off coupon as they pass within three blocks of a Subway. As designers, we need to think through the worst options possible with these features. If everyone behaves well, this stuff works fine. But not everyone behaves well. The world has some real assholes in it, and we need to design with these assholes in mind. What happens when a bad actor can track you home from the gym? What happens when some drunken douchebag leaves his own phone in an Uber so he can find out where the female driver lives using FindMy-Phone? (It's happened.) When it comes to applications and services that track our whereabouts, we need to design with assholes in mind. Sometimes they're the biggest market.

AFFILIATE CONTENT

A few days ago, I was on a news site I respect, one of the smaller sized ones without deep pockets. The kind of news site that's always having membership pledge drives so it can keep writing good stuff. I was reading an article on Donald Trump and the politics of disinformation. It was a good article. Well written. Well researched. Again, it was an article about how lying erodes trust. When I was finished reading it, I was prompted to read a selection of articles, including one about how Marcia gave the crew of *The Brady Bunch* a little more than they bargained for, with an accompanying upskirt photo of an actor playing a teenage character. I could've also opted for an article on childhood photos of history's most evil people or another about what celebrities from the '80s look like now.

This is the kind of shit written by clickbait content farms like Revcontent, Taboola, Outbrain, and more. They're deceptive, they're dangerously stupid, and they convert really well. This is bottom of the barrel advertising. As display advertising dies, site owners are getting more and more desperate to keep their revenue up. Now, solving the display advertising revenue model is beyond the mandate of this book, and certainly beyond the qualifications of its author, but it's definitely within the mission of this book to tell you that you cannot feed your readers this slop. A news site giving me information on the evils of disinformation cannot keep itself alive by doing the same. If you work at one of the dung farms that shovels this crap out, walk away. There are better ways to make a living.

"FREE SPEECH"

Congress shall make no law respecting an establishment of religion, or prohibiting the free exercise thereof; or abridging the freedom of speech, or of the press; or the right of the people peaceably to assemble, and to petition the Government for a redress of grievances.

That right there is the First Amendment of the United States in its entirety! Blessedly short, blessedly simple, and blessedly clear. These five freedoms establish the cornerstone of our society, granted in one slightly run-on sentence. Amazing.

I want to focus on the first word for a bit: Congress. Congress being the legislative branch of the US government. The first amendment says Congress shall make no laws restricting these blessed five freedoms. Now, unless you work for the government, you don't work for the government. Because of this amendment, all our national parks have sad little areas by the entrance with a little brown metal sign that says "Free Speech Area." That means that any US citizen, myself included, can go stand in front of that sign and start ranting and raving about how the animals are naked and the trees are too tall and the gift shops never have keychains with your name on them, as long as what we're raving about doesn't break some other law, like screaming about how you're going to kill the president. There are limits. We get to do that because the national parks are run by the government and according to the first amendment, the government cannot restrict our speech.

Now, if you're at work, I want you to do an exercise. (This is especially important to do if you're a Twitter employee.) Those of you not currently at work can do this the next time you're at work. Ready? Stand up. Look around. Are you currently in a national park? No? Are you in a government building? Also no? Great. Then the first amendment does not apply to you, or to the people that use your service. You do *not* need to hang a little brown metal sign that says "Free Speech Area" in your workplace. In fact, and this is the really interesting part, you are allowed to hang a "management refuses the right to service" sign in your office, as long as you don't refuse the right to serve a discriminated group. Again, there are —and should be—limits.

The first amendment was put in place to ensure that the government didn't start forcing the majority's views on us, and also to ensure that the press could tell us what the government was doing! It was not put in place to ensure that WhitePowerBob5000 could spew his racist bile to

50,000 people. We don't owe WhitePowerBob5000 jack shit. We don't owe him a platform. We don't owe him our time, and we don't owe him our protection. The people to whom we do owe all of those things are the people that WhitePowerBob5000 attacks on a daily basis. We owe it to society to uplift the voices that WhitePowerBob5000 is attempting to silence. If we truly care about free speech, let's make sure *those* voices are free. White-PowerBob5000 can go fuck himself. He is, however, free to go spew his bile in that sad little area in front of the national park. Hopefully one with large hungry bears.

You do not have to build WhitePowerBob5000 a platform.

USER-POLICING

On January 29th, 2016, Facebook banned private gun sales. They puffed up their chest, issued a press release, got tons of feel-good column inches across the globe, then told their members to get to work doing the thing they'd just taken the credit for. Facebook didn't actually take down any of the private gun sales it had just banned. It expected its members to do that work for them.

So I did. In June of that year, after the Orlando nightclub shooting where forty-nine people were murdered in an act of domestic terrorism, I joined a group of people who were reporting private gun sales on Facebook. We scoured the site. Private gun sales weren't hard to find. A simple search for "AR15" would yield dozens of results. We methodically went through a reporting flow of about five screens, a flow that was randomized so that it was never exactly the same two times in a row. We reported the sales, and waited for Facebook to take them down. About half of what we reported came back as not being a violation. We'd challenge the decision. About *half* of those came back as not being a violation.

Eventually we went public with what we were doing, both to point out that Facebook wasn't adhering to their ban, and to recruit new members for flagging these illegal sales. Me and at least one other member of the group were doxxed. My company started receiving hate calls. One person posted a photo where they were pointing a gun at my head and my son was threatened online. Bear in mind that we weren't even asking Facebook to change a policy, just to enforce an existing one.

Facebook can identify your grandmother in a photo of thirty people, shot in the dark, with your uncle standing in front of her, wearing a Blake Bortles jersey. They have some pretty smart people designing some pretty sophisticated software. They could easily make the elimination of private gun sales automated and effective. If they wanted to. When someone asks you to take on a chore they could more easily do themselves, it's generally because they don't really want to do it.

Meanwhile, Twitter, who, as we've previously discussed has to eliminate all traces of white supremacy, hate speech, and Nazi paraphernalia in order to operate in Germany, makes their users report the same violations by hand in the US. Again, they're already aware of the violations. Twitter doesn't want to bear the responsibility of policing its own platform, or the repercussions. They'll happily put that on their users. "User-flagged" is a poor substitute for leadership.

When you are designing these platforms, you cannot put the onus of enforcing policies on your users. It's one thing to flag things that fall through the cracks. Things always fall through the cracks. When your entire system for enforcing violation relies on users policing themselves, you're not doing your job responsibly.

TARGETED ADVERTISING

On September 18, 2018, *ProPublica* published an article on Facebook's targeted ad practices[32]. In an investigation of Facebook's ad practices, *ProPublica* found ninety-one recruitment ads posted by Uber. Of those ninety-one ads, eighty-seven were specifically targeted to men, one was targeted to women, and three didn't target a specific sex. It's not shocking that Silicon Valley's largest cesspool of toxic bro culture is specifically looking to hire men. In fact, my reaction when I read this was more along the lines of "of course they are" rather than indignation. Because, of course they are. According to *ProPublica*, which is very good at what it does—seriously—give them your money), Uber was one of fifteen employers they found in the past year who were buying ads on Facebook and targeting a specific group. They also point out that in 1973, the Supreme Court ruled that "it is illegal for an employer to take out job ads in newspapers with parameters such as: 'help wanted—men.'" The ACLU, among others, is currently filing a claim with the Equal Employment Opportunity Commission. Here's the fun part: they're filing the complaint against Facebook for making it possible. Remember James Liang, the VW engineer who went to jail for knowingly writing software that broke that law? That case was a harbinger of things to come. If we continue to design interfaces that knowingly break the law we have to expect it'll bite us in the ass. Not only is designing an interface that allows you to post discriminatory ads illegal, it's unethical.

Okay, now let's deal with Facebook. When ProPublica reached out to them for a comment, Facebook spokesman Joe Osborne delivered this golden chestnut of entitlement:

> *"There is no place for discrimination on Facebook; it's strictly prohibited in our policies. We look forward to defending our practices once we have an opportunity to review the complaint."*

In other words, "We're not sure what we did, but once we find out, we'll tell you how it's right." I'm sure Facebook will go on to say that it's not responsible for the ads bought on their site. Like a hoodie-clad Pontius Pilate, they'll wash their hands of the whole thing and say that if people want to post discriminatory ads on their service, a service that just happens to allow them to post discriminatory ads which just happen to break the law, how are they responsible? Well, they are—and so is every designer who worked on that ad platform. You either knew it allowed for discriminatory ads, or you didn't ask the right questions. Either way, it got through the gate on your watch.

On August 28, 2014, President Barack Obama wore a tan suit for a press conference, and America lost its collective mind. The media went into overdrive. To believe the news and the discourse online was to believe that President Obama's decision to wear a tan suit amounted to a constitutional crisis. Presidents are supposed to wear dark suits. Black. Gray. Blue. Tan was an affront to democracy itself. This discussion went on for about a week. By 2018, President Trump was paying off sex workers to remain silent about affairs, and we mostly shrugged. In less than four years, the behavior we were willing to tolerate from a sitting president took a hell of a hit. In less than four years, what we were willing to be outraged by shifted drastically.

There's a concept called an Overton window, which describes what we're willing to discuss or tolerate over time—or as the window opens or closes. What was once unthinkable (window closed) such as putting children in cages or constant surveillance or a president breaking with standards of decorum, slowly becomes policy (window open) as we get used to new behavior. Now, this isn't always a negative. Overton's window can also be applied to things such as gay marriage, Black presidents, and legal weed, all of which were once unthinkable, even in my lifetime, and have come to pass. (Though some vigilance is still required if we want to keep those windows open.) It does mean that when an idea is introduced into the public sphere, as outrageous as it may seem at the time, unless someone is willing to shut that window hard, it's on its way to acceptance. Ten years ago, if I'd asked you if you were alright with one of the world's largest corporations listening to your every conversation you have at home, you would've been horrified at the idea. If you're reading this book ten years after I've written it, you may think it quaint that we once had to say our thoughts aloud to get cat litter shipped to us.

If left unchecked, today's monsters become tomorrow's objects of comfort. If you don't believe me, please remember that your pug's ancestors used to be canine apex predators.

Obviously, this is far from a complete list and any attempt at a complete list would be wrong by the time you read this book. There are so many more monsters already in existence, so many more developing as we speak, and future monsters that we can only have nightmares about. My goal here isn't so much to give you the specific method to destroy specific unethical behavior because like all viruses, they'll mutate, and the tools we use today may not work tomorrow. The constant here can't be the method. The constant needs to be the defender. That is you.

My goal is to let you know that it's our duty to fight them. As designers, we've been charged with protecting the people who come in contact with our work.

Many of the design practices in this chapter can even live in murky legal waters. Is it legal? I don't care. Our question is whether it's ethical, and the law often drags far behind what's ethical. Is it legal to stalk someone for five minutes after they've used your app? Actually, in some places it is, and in some places it's not. That's not the point. The point is that it's wrong. A lot of the decisions we'll have to make will be judgment decisions. (We're about to enter into that murky morals or ethics area. Hold onto your butts.) Look, designers kinda live in the land of innovation. A lot of the stuff we end up working on will be new and weird and different, and that's not always bad! It's also not always good. More importantly, there's often no precedent for it, so you're gonna have to make some calls. Put on the brakes, gather people together—people who don't all look like or have the same experiences as you—and walk through the possible ramifications of what you're being asked to make. If it doesn't pass that test? Do not make it.

"But Mike, the decision to include some of this stuff is made beyond my pay grade!" is a thing said by people who've never actually tried to fight something above their pay grade. Also, it's bullshit. Making ethical calls on what goes on the interface is exactly what you are being paid to do. So, if you're not doing it, you're actually not doing your job. You're as much of a stakeholder as anyone in that building. You have agency and as we said back in an earlier chapter, you were hired for your counsel. Give it.

When monsters knock, we need to be the ones who knock back.

Persuading People Is Easy

.

That's a pixel.

Or rather, the print approximation of a pixel. But you get the idea. It's tiny. So tiny I'm afraid it may not print well. So here's another one just to make sure:

.

A pixel. It's the smallest unit of measurement you can design in. So stupidly insignificant, it's nothing. Yet, designers take great pride in unironically referring to themselves as pixelpushers. We push the pixels. We color the pixels. We animate the pixels. We coat pixels in meaning. We count how many pixels we can see on our screens. We are obsessed with mastering the smallest possible thing we can work with. Worst of all, when we encounter a problem, our first reaction is to rearrange our pixels, as if some magic reordering will render us a different reaction. This arranging of pixels is one of the first things we learn to do as designers. Sadly, for many of us, the job ends where it begins—by gaining expertise and mastery over the smallest unit of measurement in design. Pushing a pixel is the absolute least you can accomplish as a designer.

A few months ago, I was giving a talk somewhere, and there were about 500 people in the audience. The talk was about design ethics. In fact, it was the precursor to this very book, meaning you're getting the talk plus more. I went over the importance of behaving ethically, gave examples of how we hadn't in the past and what those effects had been, and then gave them some solutions. I'm sure I also made fun of Jack Dorsey because, c'mon. Anyway, the talk went well. There was applause, which is always nice, and afterward, people came up to me and told me they learned a lot, which is also nice. The reason I'm bringing it up is because one of those very nice, very pleasant people who came up to me afterward also asked me a well-meaning question that frankly kind of rattled me.

"Do you ever miss designing?"

Do I ever miss designing? Quite honestly, I didn't think I'd ever stopped designing. Here I was giving a talk about design ethics. I'm writing about design all the time. I do workshops with designers. I help clients solve problems all the time. All of this is design to me. In my own mind, I was evolving as a designer. (Or maybe that was just the story I was telling myself.) So when he asked me if I missed designing, I was taken aback and replied "What do you mean? I'm designing all the time!"

"No, I mean making things. You know... with pixels."

That's when I understood. A lot of designers equate designing with the pushing of pixels. (So do the people who hire us.) We equate our power with the ability to move this tiniest of units into proper and pleasing placements. We still believe this to be our one true purpose. This, and only this, is design work. Thus everything I was currently doing wasn't design work, but rather things keeping me from doing true design work.

We've also been taught to persuade people by how well we can position pixels. (Let your work speak *for* you!) When people push back on our solutions, we react by pushing pixels to other new places, as if persuasion happens at the pixel level. We equate our jobs with aesthetics and while aesthetics are certainly a component of design, they're truly just a small component. A tiny bit. The smallest bit possible.

We need to care much more about the effects of our work than the cleverness of our pixel positioning. If we want to truly influence what we're designing, and to have a say in how things are *truly* designed, not to mention who we affect, we need to expand our understanding of what design means. We need to expand what we're capable of affecting, from tiny little dots to people's minds.

To design is to influence.

The important work won't get done at the pixel level. A pixel is just a point of proof in the stage of execution. It's the period at the end of the sentence. That sentence though? That's the important thing. To design is to influence people. To design is to build new connections in people's minds. To design is to build relationships where there previously weren't any.

True design decisions are made face-to-face. They are made in meetings where you need to be. They are made in the hallways you need to patrol. They are made when people interact with each other. The first design decision on your project was made when a budget was allocated. Sadly, a lot of design decisions get made in places that haven't granted you access—yet. We need to change that.

It's time to move beyond pixel into argument. If we truly want to influence what our labor is being used for, we need to start pushing *people* into proper and pleasing placements. If we truly want to influence what our labor is being used for, we are going to have to do it with our voices. We need to focus less about where our pixels are placed, and to focus more on where our bodies are placed. If we want to design the right way, we are going to have to do it by talking to people. We are not pixel pushers. We are the defense against monsters.

Fear us, because we will not let shit through those gates.

HUMILITY IS EXPENSIVE

When I was a kid, my well-meaning immigrant mother told me to keep my head down. When I was in school, the Sisters of Saint Joseph taught me the meek would inherit the earth. When I was a young designer, my professors taught me good work would sell itself.

With respect to my mother, and my mother only, all that advice was bullshit.

Like many designers, I spent the beginning of my career using the humble approach, hoping that at some point someone would notice that I was good at what I did; hoping the work would get noticed, hoping that I'd made the work so obviously clear that I wouldn't have to advocate for it. It never happened. Finally, my frustration at seeing good work thrown in the garbage can overcame my fear of speaking up. Because that's what it was, fear. Humility is just lipstick on a pig called fear.

If you've hired me to do good work, I owe it to you and more importantly, the people that work is going to affect to do good work. I also need to tell you why the work is good, to walk you through all its aspects, and to explain to you how I reached the conclusion that the work is good. My confidence in the work then passes from me to you and puts that work one step closer to helping the people it's intended to help. My confidence isn't for my benefit or even my boss's benefit, it's for the people's benefit. When we see them as the reason for our confidence, then humility isn't just expensive, it's also selfish. How dare you allow your fear to keep people from being helped.

Our profession needs to be willing to speak truth to power. We need to say no, ask why, and check receipts. We need to advocate for the people who aren't in the room and stand up to those who are. That's the job. We must be engaged in the process of what gets designed way before it enters the phase we've traditionally (and erroneously) thought of as design. We're going to need to raise our voices.

None of this can happen if we're being humble. Humility is a trait we simply don't have the luxury of entertaining. Too many people are counting on us.

Strong caveat: confidence is not the same as cockiness. Confidence is about the work. It means I've done the math, crossed my t's, dotted my i's, and listened to feedback. Cockiness is about ego. It means I don't think I have to do any of those things. Cockiness got us to the garbage fire we find ourselves in today.

BE WILLING TO GET FIRED

There's a whole chapter coming up about this, and I mentioned it earlier, but I need to include it here as well because a willingness to get fired needs to be your baseline state if you want to persuade people. Unless you walk into a situation willing to get fired for doing good work, you're holding back. If your priority is to save your own neck, you're gonna hold back. You'll be constantly looking for the line. Will bringing up a particular topic get me fired? Will pointing out that this software we've spent a year on has serious harmful flaws get me fired? Will it cost our team its bonuses? (I've seen teams deliver shit to make a bonus date.) Will fighting to take care of our users' well-being hamper my career advancement? (Would you want to advance in a job where it did?) Will refusing to work on software that lies to our customers get me fired? Will refusing to bring up the fact that our users are constantly harassed and abused get me fired?

How much better would the world be if everyone in those situations decided they were willing to get fired for doing the right thing? How many times has someone refused to do the right thing out of fear of getting fired?

There are more jobs out there; don't let a job stop you from doing something worthwhile with your life.

GET IN THE ROOM

There's an activity I like to do with young designers. It's about chairs. (Designers like chairs almost as much as they like glasses.) I pull out the rattiest-looking chair I can find and I ask them how they can make the chair more comfortable. Some of them suggest adding a cushion to the seat of the chair. Some of them suggest a cushion to the seat and the back. Some of them suggest adding arms. Some of them suggest sitting in the chair a different way. Some of them suggest sawing the legs off the chair to make it closer to the ground. Eventually they come to the realization that all they're doing is making the chair slightly more tolerable and potentially even more ratty looking. Then someone makes the magical breakthrough: "The only way to make the chair more comfortable is to go back in time to when the chair was being first discussed." Bingo!

If you want to have a say in what's being designed you need to be in the room where design decisions are being made. By design decisions, I mean things like metrics, strategy, outcomes, definitions, timelines, and resources. All of those things will influence what is being designed a million times more than where pixels ultimately get placed.

Oh, but you don't get invited to those discussions? For the record, every time a designer tells me this, I follow up with, "Have you ever asked to be in those discussions?" and half the time the answer is no. At which point, I have to take a deep breath. First off, no one is going to invite you to those conversations on their own. Remember, they don't know what it takes to design something correctly. They think they hired a pixel pusher. Don't fall into the trap of behaving like one. Only you know what it takes for you to do your job correctly. They hired you to do a job, you have to tell them what you need in order to do it well. If part of that is being part of these conversations—and it is—then you need to make the case for being in those meetings.

"I'm a designer. Please allow me to do the job I was hired to do. You're going to be making decisions in this meeting which impact design and I need to be there. Finding out about this stuff afterward is going to cost us all time and money and possibly take us down some bad paths. I can help by being in the room."

Let's deal with the *real* reason we don't ask to be in these conversations. They are boring. At least, they're often boring. I get that. You'd rather be doing something else. You'd rather be pushing pixels around on your giant monitor while listening to the new *War on Drugs* on your expensive headphones. I would too. But then shit hits our desk. We look through it.

We partially understand it. We may even want to discuss it, which is more difficult now because all the decision-makers will tell you the time for discussion came and went. So, we roll our eyes and we execute it. That's a shitty way to do the job. We're defenders, remember? Mind the gate.

You may not get in the room the first time you ask. So ask again. Make yourself a nuisance about it. Eventually they might relent just to shut you up. That's fine. It gets you in the room. What's the worst thing that can happen? They fire you from a job they weren't allowing you to do anyway.

MAKE THE ARGUMENT

If you want to persuade people, you're going to have to learn what they care about. Your boss probably doesn't want a thirty-minute lesson on typography during a design presentation that took three weeks to schedule and for which she's skipping her lunch. When you're able to get time with the people who make decisions that affect millions of people, you're going to have to use that time wisely. You need to know how to get their attention immediately, how to make sure they understand why you need their attention, and most importantly, how to make sure they know what you need from them.

For example: "If we launch an ad tool that lets you target users by race, we're going to get someone killed," is gonna get your bosses' attention better than, "I have some concerns about our new ad tool." It also just got you five more minutes of their time. Now, you have to figure out how to use those five minutes.

I've seen way too many designers present their arguments with incredibly long lead-ins. They're trying to justify their work, lay the groundwork, show their process, and end with a big reveal. This is exhausting. It takes forever to get to. It bores people. No one cares about your process. No one wants to sit through twenty minutes of background.

In my presentation workshop, I have participants get up to do five-minute presentations. I've started assigning one of the participants to get up at the one-minute mark, and walk out the door. After the presentation is over, they come back in, and tell us what they heard. It's usually nothing of value. This may sound cruel, but if you've ever had a key decision maker walk out of your presentation early you know what I'm talking about. It happens all the time. Most of the workshop participants want to know what they can do to change the boss's behavior. In truth, it's much easier to change your own.

There's a metaphor used in journalism called the inverted pyramid. In short, you give the most important information at the very beginning, increase the details as, or if, the reader continues reading the article, and then finish up with relevant background. If you've ever read the headline to a story and decided you already knew everything you wanted to know, now you know why. It's by design. The inverted pyramid moves the reveal, which you've been saving up for the big finish, right to the top.

So, the next time you want to convince people they're making shitty software that might get people killed, start by telling them they're making shitty software that might get people killed. Then tell them why. Then tell them how you can keep that from happening.

I guarantee they'll stick around just a bit longer and possibly even for the whole thing.

MAKE ALLIES

Persuading people means building alliances. You're gonna need people in your corner. Which means you're going to need people skills. It's okay. People are easy. They basically all want the same thing. They want to be listened to and respected. Sound familiar? Yeah, that's what you want too. That's what we all want. Turns out we have a lot in common. Start there.

Building alliances is easier than it sounds as my friend, Dan Ryan, head of tech at Ragtag, says, "sometimes an alliance is as simple as acknowledging someone else's work and value, and making sure that others are noticing it, too."

The higher you climb the design ladder and the closer you get to where decisions are being made, the more important people skills are going to be.

Yes, this is all design. The person who convinces the boss that you need more time for research has done more to influence the design of the product than the person placing the pixels by a long shot.

My friend Anna Pickard, who's in charge of brand communication at Slack, puts it this way:

"I listen to people and provide them with what they need. I listen to what they're not saying and provide them with that as well, or at least have it in hand, if that's what they actually wanted. I unblock things. I help people find the people they need in order to get the thing they need done, done. But I don't see any of that as building alliances. What they need from me, or from each other, in one instance will not be what (or who) they need next time. I embed myself by becoming the warp to people's weft."

"But Mike, I'm an introvert." That's cute. Let me tell you a secret: so am I. I enjoy sitting in my living room reading a book more than I enjoy being out with people. I like going to the movies by myself. I avoid crowded places. Being invited to weddings and other social events fills me with anxiety. For years, that's how I behaved at work. I sat in the corner. I made the work I was told to make. I rolled my eyes when I thought I was being asked to do something dumb. I complained that no one was listening to me. Then I realized the reason no one was listening to me was because I never said anything! I had to learn how to be an extrovert, at least at work. Speaking up is part of the job. Some of us are natural extroverts, but the rest of us have to work at it. Getting the job done and speaking up to people and building alliances are gonna require you to push past that level of discomfort, at least at work. You can still be an introvert at home.

Here's what my friend, accessibility evangelist, Elle Waters had to say on it: "I spent a lot of my professional career getting people to give a damn about people with disabilities mostly by making alliances. So, I quickly found that the most important way to do that was to focus on what was valuable to them. To me, being actively interested in other people's success is a clear way to build an alliance." Elle put herself out there, not because she's a natural extrovert, but because she understands that she's the advocate for those people with disabilities. If she doesn't go into "extrovert mode," she's not getting those people the help they deserve.

If you believe there's a problem at work, you're probably not the only one. (And if you are, it might be time to leave.) Find the people who agree with you or who can be swayed. Find the people willing to have the discussion. Whose eyes lit up when you brought up an issue at a meeting? Who was paying more attention than usual to what you had to say? Who asked follow-up questions? Reach out to them. Use those people skills.

On July 26, 2018, Microsoft CEO Satya Nadella took the stage at an employee event. During the Q&A session, employees questioned him about Microsoft's contract with ICE (Immigration and Customs Enforcement). After ICE started separating children from their parents at the border and caging them, Microsoft employees were aghast that ICE was using its products for processing data and artificial intelligence capabilities (i.e. facial recognition). They banded together and put together a petition with 300,000 signatures, including 500 Microsoft employees, demanding that Microsoft kill the contract. During that Q&A session on July 26, 2018, a Microsoft employee presented their CEO with a USB stick containing the petition and the signatures. Microsoft has 135,000 employees. It took less than one percent of Microsoft employees to make a difference.

Was that employee terrified to do that? I'm guessing more than a little. But that employee was presenting that petition on behalf of 500 allies. They banded together because they didn't want the products of their labor being used to put children in cages. Were they afraid of retribution? Getting fired? Careers derailed? I'm sure more than a few of them were. I'm sure the decision to sign that petition wasn't taken lightly. I'm also pretty sure that with the addition of every name on that petition, the decision to sign got a little easier. The more allies we gather, the braver we feel. That's human nature. We're pack mammals. We feel more secure in groups. That doesn't make us weak, it makes us human. Find your group. Remember, they want the same thing you do. They want respect. They want be heard. And they want to do the right thing. Remember that, and you'll have no trouble making allies.

"I DON'T KNOW"

During my workshops I like to ask people a question: What's the most confident statement that can come out of your mouth?

"I got this."

"I know what to do."

"I'm right!"

Then, and this is how I know if the workshop is going well, there'll be a tentative voice from the back and it's usually someone who hasn't said much all day, someone who was doing more listening than talking.

"I don't know?" And yeah, they usually frame it as a question, but I know they don't mean it as a question.

"You, in the back! What did you just say?"

"I don't know."

"Correct!"

At some point, as much as you may have prepared and practiced, the person you're attempting to persuade will ask you a question that stumps you. (This moment is where careers are made, by the way!)

You have a few options here:

• You can lie, but only assholes lie.

• You can try to make something up on the fly, but they'll see right through that. Plus, it'll probably be wrong, in which case, it's a lie.

• You can buy for time with a strategically stretched out series of ummmmmmms until a co-worker bails you out. But every ummmmmmmm that comes out of your mouth is decreasing the room's confidence in you. Or, or, OR! You can say the most confident thing that has ever come out of your mouth: "I don't know."

Also, you need to follow that up with something like, "I'm excited to find out," or, "Give me until the end of the day/week to look into it," and make sure you do.

It's easy to look confident when you know what you're talking about. (To be clear, you should know what you're talking about most of the time.) But letting people know that you're confident enough to admit that you're at a loss is when you beat the level boss. No one has all the answers, and pretending you do doesn't make you look confident; it makes you look like a fool.

Being calm and collected while expressing a missing piece of knowledge? Amazing. Confident. If anything, people's confidence in you has grown. Now they trust you. They know you'll admit when you don't know something. They know you won't lie to them, and that's huge.

DATA IS FOR PEOPLE WHO NEVER WENT TO CHURCH

Hi. Let's piss some people off by talking about vaccines.

The measles vaccine was introduced to the United States in the 60's, and then in 1971 it was rolled into MMR vaccine. Measles is the first M, the second M is mumps, and the R is Rubella. That's probably how you got the vaccine as a kid. Your first cocktail!

According to the CDC, prior to the vaccine, 3 to 4 million people in the United States were infected per year. 48,000 were hospitalized, and 400 to 500 died.[33] Those numbers are yearly. By 1981, the measles vaccine had reduced those numbers by eighty percent. At this point, the CDC began recommending a second dose. In 2000, the CDC declared the measles epidemic eliminated in the United States. There's data for all of this. Go online, check out CDC.gov. They've got piles of data. This story can end right here as a raging success: There was a problem. Smart people designed a cure, and put it in a vaccine. We all got a shot plus a lollipop, and everyone lived happily ever after.

To be fair, measles wasn't *totally* eliminated in the United States. There were always a few cases here and there, usually around fifty a year or so. In 2014, however, the CDC reported 667 cases of measles. Why? According to Jane Seward, CDC deputy director of the Division of Viral Diseases, as quoted in The Atlantic:[34]

> *"The vast majority of our cases every single year are unvaccinated people who choose not to be vaccinated. They are living in a family who are unvaccinated and they have friends who are unvaccinated. They might go to a school with a high proportion of people who are unvaccinated."*

People stopped believing the data. Somewhere between when the measles vaccine was first made available and when our collective memory of children dying from the measles had passed into legend, we stopped believing the data. Despite a total lack of data, parents started believing the vaccine was actually dangerous to their children. Why? Because people are not data-driven mammals. People make decisions based on feelings and emotion more than they make decisions based on data. I'm guilty of this myself.

Silicon Valley claims to be obsessed with data. (I blame *Moneyball*.) Take a look through any of the Silicon Valley rags or the tech section of the three newspapers still standing and you'll see about three stories a day on data. How to get it. What to do with it. Who's selling it to whom. Who needs it. How to protect yours. We've collected more data in the last ten years than we can process in the next hundred. No one can exactly remember why we're collecting it, but everyone's afraid to stop. Yet, with all this data at our disposal, we've created a garbage fire run by platforms of vitriol. Here's some more data: we're idiots.

Like any good designer, I work with data. If you're designing something for people to use and no one can use it, that's data. You'd be a fool to ignore the data. If I'm hired to fix a system that's been in place for a few years, I've probably got a few years of data to study, and I'd be an idiot to ignore it. (Just like parents would be idiots to ignore decades of data on measles vaccines.) While you're designing, you're like a scientist. You study every data point. It's the smart thing to do. Then you gotta persuade people the work is right. Hold onto your butts...

The minute you put a design solution in front of data-driven Silicon Valley types, they start talking about feelings.

"This *feeeeeels* wrong."

"I'm not *feeeeeling* it."

"Oh, I like the *feel* of this!"

It's a little crazy-making, but it's also understandable. I told you people don't make decisions based on data; they make them based on feelings. For the record, men have so many more feelings than women do. We make *all* our decisions based on feelings; we just lie and say it's data. Want proof? Watch a guy buy a TV sometime.

So, while you should absolutely include the study of data in your approach, recognize that when you get to the point where you're trying to persuade someone about good work, you need a story. Work like a scientist but present like a snake-charmer. When I'm trying to persuade someone, I start by painting a picture in the person's mind. There's a future where you do what's right, and I paint that rosy. There's a future where you do what's wrong, and I paint that dismally. My goal is to get you to walk into that rosier future, the one where everything works out. If you want to persuade someone, you need to take them on a little journey. Think of all the things that have ever persuaded you in your life. Think of all the memorable speeches you've seen. Think of how they moved you. Those people did the work. They collected the data. Then they used it to tell a story.

If you're not persuading people, you're not telling a good enough story.

When to Throw Your Body on the Gears

On September 3, 2018, Georgia Wells and Kristen Grind published an article in the *Wall Street Journal* called *Twitter's Long, Slow Struggle to Police Bad Actors*.

The article was posted right before Twitter CEO Jack Dorsey was scheduled to speak before Congress about suspicious political content, privacy, and general bad behavior. (Irony noted.) According to the article, and as told to the writers by Twitter executives, "Twitter relies primarily on its users to report abuses and has a consistent set of policies so that decisions aren't made by just one person."

Once users flag a post, it supposedly goes to a group that makes a decision about whether that content and/or user gets booted. Here's where it starts getting interesting. The article then goes on to report, according to inside sources, that Jack Dorsey frequently overrules the findings of that group. I quote:

> *Last month, after Twitter's controversial decision to allow far-right conspiracy theorist Alex Jones to remain on its platform, Mr. Dorsey told one person that he had overruled a decision by his staff to kick Mr. Jones off, according to a person familiar with the discussion.*

To be fair, Alex Jones was eventually kicked off Twitter right after those same Congressional hearings. Right after he got in Jack Dorsey's face and chewed him out. The timing speaks volumes. It appears that Jack *does* care about harassment and abuse. His own.

The article then goes on to talk about how Twitter's own employees are frustrated about their company's inability to follow its own rules for what is and isn't abusive content.

> *Twitter's initial inaction on Mr. Jones, after several other major tech companies banned or limited his content, drew fierce backlash from the public and Twitter's own employees, some of whom tweeted in protest.*

I have no doubt that employees at Twitter are frustrated about how their company is being run. Same goes for employees at Facebook, Google, and even Uber. To think there aren't at least some people trying to do the right thing at these companies is naive. The question isn't whether they're there. It's why they stay.

Why don't Twitter employees quit?

Why don't Facebook employees strike?

Why didn't Uber employees run Travis Kalanick out of town on a rail?

According to that article, Twitter employees attempted to do the right thing. They attempted to do the job they were hired for, and then they were undermined by management. I sympathize with how frustrating that must be. At the same time, when you are hired to do a job, you need to do it. Especially when you know it's the right thing to do.

Sometimes we'll have to fight to design the right thing. Like we've mentioned already, sometimes people just need a little persuading. The goal is to work at a place where the latter is true—a workplace where people are driven by higher goals, mutual respect for one another, and a desire to make the world a better place. Unfortunately, at this moment in time, most jobs in Silicon Valley (as well as other places that Silicon Valley has begun to infect) are places where the former is true—we're gonna have to fight to do good work.

There will be times when you have to walk away or throw your body on the gears. Your job is to keep bad work from happening. If we can do it through persuasion, fantastic. Get *really* good at persuading people, because the alternatives aren't easy. They sometimes include a great personal cost, which isn't to say that cost should be avoided. In fact, it's sometimes unavoidable, but not standing up to do the right thing needs to become unthinkable.

The stain of bad decision-making gets everywhere. At some point, the fault passes from leadership, who's giving bad orders, to the rank and file who keep following them. They cannot keep doing these things without you! At some point, you need to realize not just the power you have to stop bad work from happening, but also the culpability of not doing so. Ultimately, the fault is neither in the order givers *nor* in our stars, but in ourselves.

There are things worth quitting for. There are things worth getting fired for. This is the time for good trouble.

WHY FIGHTING IS HARD

Let's address some real concerns. I am writing this book in the United States, the majority of people who read it will be in the United States, and the majority of the companies we're discussing in this book are in the United States.

To live and work in the United States is to live and work in the last rich nation that doesn't provide its citizens access to health care. In the United States, the majority of workers are offered health insurance by their employers. It may or may not be fully paid by the employer, that's their call. According to Forbes, the percentage of companies that fully cover their employees' health insurance has decreased from thirty-four percent in 2001 to nine percent in 2016.[35] That's just counting the companies on their *100 Best Companies to Work For* list. The entire system is shameful. It's shameful for many reasons, but for the purposes of this book, I want to focus on one of those reasons.

Let's say I work at Twitter, and my job is to decide who's broken our rules. Let's say, for example, that I've decided Alex Jones has broken our rules, which is a decision that falls under my job description to make, but my employer decides to undermine me. I now have two options. I can either go along with what I'm being told to do, which would be the unethical thing to do, because I have evidence that Alex Jones is harassing people and has *indeed* broken our rules. Or, I can do the ethical thing, fight to do my job, and have Alex Jones banned. Except… except… I have a small child with a health problem and she's on my insurance, which my employer provides. I cannot fault someone for choosing their kid in that situation. The problem here isn't someone making an unethical decision, although they are. The problem is the system which puts a worker in that position.

We must be free to do our jobs, and to do them as they need to be done without our family's healthcare hanging over our heads. To understand the reasons why people who might *want* to do the right thing don't always choose to do it, we need to understand the entire system in which they work. Health care is a huge part of it. Education is another.

Again, I must ask my international readers to withhold their audible gasps. In the United States, according to the College Board, the average cost of tuition and fees for the 2017-2018 school year at a private college is $34,740. A public college will cost you an average of $9,970 if you already live in that state, and $25,620 if you live out-of-state. Multiply that by the four years it'll take you to get your degree (if you're focused and/or can get into all the classes you need to graduate) and you've got a ton of people in their early twenties entering the workforce saddled with sixty to eighty grand in debt. In 1996, the Federal Reserve estimated that the average monthly student loan payment is $393. Those numbers aren't just high, they're a form of violence on young people. America punishes young people for wanting to learn. This needs to change.

This sets up scenarios where people entering the workforce need to find jobs that pay them well, and once they've found that job, they need to keep it. So, we've got young kids with very little job experience working at these massive companies that pay them enough to pay down that student debt *and* are supplying their health insurance. This is not a good recipe for an ethical revolution. This is a recipe for how to build a workforce that's beholden to you.

Because let's also remember that most of the states in America practice at-will employment, which means your boss can fire you for any reason, at any time. (All my readers in Scandinavia just passed out.) Some professions have either unions or professional organizations to help mitigate this and to bargain collectively. Designers do not. This needs to change.

This problem is only worse for international workers here on work visas. I recently spoke to Heather Champ, who did community management at Flickr for years—and was damn good at it! She had this to say:

"Let's say Facebook is bringing you over and you're on some sort of visa. If you lose your job, you immediately have to leave the country and that's going to have a big impact on how much you're going to push back on something. You know, I initially started working in the US on a NAFTA visa and if I lost my job, I had two weeks to leave the country. That's going to have a big impact on whether or not I'm going to push back."

That's heartbreaking and real.

Just so we're clear, neither our horrific health care system, nor educational debt, nor immigration status, absolve you from doing your job ethically; and nor do they make it okay to work unethically. I do, however, empathize with those situations, and my advice would be that if you're encumbered by a need to pay off student loans or to care for health needs of family members, to avoid working at places where you'll have to fight too much. Meanwhile, join us in solving the health care, student debt, and immigration problem at the polls.

GOLDEN HANDCUFFS ARE STILL HANDCUFFS

A friend of mine once told me that it's harder to stay and advocate for doing the right thing than to quit. I agree, as long as there's still a chance that advocacy is working. After all, this is the job we were hired to do—to advocate. We don't walk away when it gets hard. We earn our money when it gets hard. So while there's a chance that our counsel will still be heeded, we stay and fight.

Before we go lighting our Molotovs, getting ready to cut the company's trunk line, and adding MDMA to the kombucha taps in the lunchroom, let's take a deep breath. The best, most effective, way for you to effect change is to stay and fight. Persuade others. Present good solutions, and fight for them.

We don't walk away when things get hard. We walk away when things get impossible. My goal here is to affect change, not to cause mass unemployment.

Sadly, I don't think our biggest problem is people giving up too quickly, but rather people not recognizing when impossible hits them in the face. Too often our old friend Overton opens the window just a bit, and the thing that horrifies us on Monday becomes acceptable by Wednesday. Sometimes, it comes with a little pay raise or an extra benefit. Sometimes the idea of not living life in the manner in which we've grown accustomed replaces our conscience. That's when we start convincing ourselves that we're affecting change from the inside, even as we're being bulldozed or ignored at every corner.

Golden handcuffs are *still* handcuffs. If something is unethical at fifteen dollars an hour, it is still unethical at a hundred and fifty dollars an hour. If something is unethical at the office, it's still unethical if they let you work from home. Riding a hi-tech wifi enabled tech bus to work doesn't change the ethics of where you're being dropped off. Beware of trading in your ethics for petty perks.

As we already discussed, there are no ethical offsets. No amount of donations to the ACLU will offset working at Palantir. As a company, no amount of employee time given to good causes offsets running a platform of harassment and abuse.

So, if you're staying and fighting, make sure you're fighting. Lest Overton's window get slammed on your fingers.

IS SABOTAGE ETHICAL?

In 1944, the CIA (or technically, the OSS, its precursor) published one of the greatest design manuals of all time, and by far my personal favorite. The *Simple Sabotage Field Manual*[36] was clandestinely, and I hope very carefully, distributed to people living in Axis or Axis-controlled countries who sided with the Allied cause, including our good friends and role models in the French Resistance. It was declassified in 2008. The manual is filled with dozens of little tips and tricks about how you can sabotage your workplace in ways that won't be too obvious. (You can do a lot more sabotage if you're not getting caught.) Why do I call it a design manual? Because, like we've discussed before, design is the solution to a problem within a set of constraints. We have a problem: Nazis. We have a solution: sabotage. We have constraints: don't get caught. It's a design manual. Among the highlights are:

- *Bring up irrelevant issues as frequently as possible.*

- *Refer back to matters decided upon at the last meeting and attempt to re-open the question of the advisability of that decision.*

- *To lower morale and with it, production, be pleasant to inefficient workers; give them undeserved promotions.*

- *Hold conferences when there is more critical work to be done.*

- *Never pass on your skill and experience to a new or less skillful worker.*

And my personal favorite:

- *Act stupid.*

Reading these, I wonder if Silicon Valley hasn't accidentally been following this manual of sabotage for the past thirty years.

So, is sabotage ethical? If you got the right lessons out of *Raiders of the Lost Ark*, you realize that the Axis (Nazis and friends) were the bad guys and the Allies are the good guys. So, this is a manual for sabotaging bad guys, and I'd argue that Nazis are about as bad as you can get on the bad guy scale. In fact, I'm not even gonna argue that. I'm just gonna call it a universal truth. Nazis were/are hateful fucks, and sabotaging their work isn't just ethical, but is your duty as a good human being. Now, I'm not going to do the thing where I compare the place you work to a Nazi-run factory or office. That's a little bombastic even for me. The question on the table is whether sabotage is ethical, so let's pull back a bit.

It's worth noting that this manual was being distributed to people who mostly couldn't leave their jobs. Some of them were actual prisoners, some of them were in prison-like circumstances. All of them were in danger. In some cases, the punishment for walking away would've been death. Obviously, the punishment for sabotage, had they been caught, would've been just as horrible. In this scenario, I'd say sabotage was ethical. When your only option is doing unethical work or death, sabotage is ethical.

You, however, *can* leave your job. So, while we may agree that sabotage is ethical, I'd have to ask you why you're sticking around a place that does unethical work. Maybe it's the health care and student loans. Fair enough. Just be honest with yourself that you're making that call. Don't confuse an inconvenience with a constraint. This may not be a good time for you to leave your job and those reasons may be well and good, but you are still making a choice.

Sabotage is an ethical option when a better option isn't available to you. When it's a matter of wanting to live in the manner in which you're accustomed, then no, sabotage isn't ethical. It's passive aggressive, at best. For example, "I want to do *something*, but I really like getting this big fat paycheck." Then no, sabotage isn't ethical. It's a way to justify the biweekly tug at the teat of unethical profit while wearing your *Stay woke* shirt to Sunday brunch.

At best, sabotage slows things down, sometimes to a molasses-like pace. Its effects are to delay the inevitable or to buy time until something changes. It's worth noting that the people following the *Simple Sabotage Field Manual* were, literally, waiting for the cavalry to show up. They were throwing a monkey wrench in the means of production until the Allies came over the hill. At which point, the Allies would destroy the means completely. (Minus a few rocket engineers that they absconded with for their own purposes. Turns out there were never actually any good guys, just people who were on the better side of history for a slight bit.)

WHEN TO PUT DOWN YOUR TOOLS

Oakland sits across the bay from San Francisco. It has a much lower median income ($52k a year vs. $96k a year). Yet, because of the influx of high-paid tech workers, it is one of the most expensive areas of the country to live. The average one-bedroom apartment in Oakland rents for about $2,680 a month. Two bedroom apartments (you know, for families) go for over $3,300 a month. A teacher's salary in Oakland starts at about $46k a year. If you had a good teacher, you can quickly see the math doesn't add up.[37]

In 2017, the teachers' contract expired. Their union asked the school district for a twelve percent pay raise over three years. They also asked for more support staff (counselors, nurses, psychologists, and special education teachers) and smaller class sizes to help them do their jobs, which is to teach kids. The teachers worked in good faith for eighteen months while a new contract was negotiated.

On February 21, 2018, with negotiations at a standstill, Oakland teachers put down their tools and stopped going to work. The people rallied around them. Seven days later, the school district agreed to an eleven percent raise over three years, slightly smaller class sizes, and raises for support staff.

There is a time to put down the tools.

If there's one thing I want you to walk away from this book realizing, just one thing, it's how much power you have in these situations. I hope that by this point, I've convinced you that you aren't just a pair of hands. You're hired to give as much counsel as labor. The minute your counsel is no longer being heeded, your labor needs to stop as well. Otherwise, you're doing half the job.

This shit that's destroying the world is being made with our labor. They can't make it without our labor. They need us! That gives us power. We have agency and we are a collective force. We are fucking legion!

When your labor is being used to unethical ends, you must put down your tools. When your labor is being used to spread inequality, you must put down your tools. When your tools are being used to take away people's humanity, you must put down your tools.

I often wonder if the employees at Twitter, Facebook, 4chan, or any of the other places that have to deal with (or fail to deal with) harassment and abuse on their platforms have mentally drawn a line in the sand for themselves. Is there a point where they'd put down the tools? Do they know where their line is? Is there a point where what they're being asked to design finally gets them to put the tools down? It wasn't when Donald Trump wasn't kicked off the service despite breaking all their rules. It wasn't when Mike Cernovich started tweeting out anti-Semitic remarks without repercussions. It wasn't when Alex Jones started doxxing the parents of murdered children without repercussions. None of those situations were enough for Twitter employees to put down their tools. So if Twitter employees do have a breaking point, we know those things weren't it.

Know where your line is, know what it would take for you to put down your tools, because it has an effect. Your company cannot make work without workers. Also know what corrective action it would take for you to pick those tools back up.

If they refuse to take that corrective action? Well, we have another step we can take...

WHEN TO BURN IT ALL DOWN

On December 2, 1964, at the height of the civil rights struggle, Mario Savio climbed the steps of Sproul Hall at the UC Berkeley, which had just banned all political activity and fundraising on campus. This is the famous last paragraph of the speech he gave that day:

There's a time when the operation of the machine becomes so odious, makes you so sick at heart, that you can't take part! You can't even passively take part! And you've got to put your bodies upon the gears and upon the wheels… upon the levers, upon all the apparatus, and you've got to make it stop! And you've got to indicate to the people who run it, to the people who own it, that unless you're free, the machine will be prevented from working at all!

There comes a time when despite our best efforts, despite the persuasion, the fighting, and the best of all possible efforts of good people, things cannot be saved. The foundation is broken. Those in charge are rotten. The effort it would take to fix something, even if everyone could decide on how to fix it, wouldn't be worth the time and investment. Or worst, a product is so inherently broken, evil, and run by unethical people that its very onerous existence only serves to further toxify society.

Not everything can be fixed. There is a time to burn things down.

The promise of the internet was that it was going to give voice to the voiceless, visibility to the invisible, and power to the powerless. That's what originally excited me about it. That's what originally excited a ton of people about it. It was supposed to be an engine of equality. Suddenly, everyone could tell their story. Suddenly, everyone could sing their song. Suddenly, that one weird kid in Helena, Montana could find another weird kid just like them in Bakersfield, California and they could talk and know they weren't alone. Suddenly, we didn't need anybody's permission to publish. We put our stories and songs and messages and artwork where the world could find them. For a while it was beautiful, it was messy, and it was punk as fuck. We all rolled up our sleeves and helped to build it.

We were the ones who were supposed to guide it there.

We failed.

We failed because we were naive enough to believe everyone had the same goals we did. We failed because we underestimated greed. We failed because we didn't pay attention to history. We failed because our definition of we wasn't big enough.

We designed and built platforms that undermined democracy across the world. That is odious.

We designed and built technology that is used to round up immigrants and refugees and put them in cages. That is odious.

We designed and built platforms that young, stupid, hateful men use to demean and shame women. That is odious.

We designed and built an entire industry that exploits the poor in order to make old rich men even richer. That is odious.

We pointed out that all these things were odious, but we were told that they were making money, so chill out. Then we became sick at heart.

If your reply is that we didn't design and build these things to be used this way, then all I can say is that you've done a shit job of designing them, because that is what they're being used for. These monsters are yours, regardless of what your intentions might have been. I realize we can't control every way that people use the tools we build, but that doesn't make us any less responsible for them. I realize you didn't build these monsters on your own, but regardless of how many people's parts your monster is made from, the fingerprints will always be your own.

The machine we've built is odious. Not only can we not participate in its operation, nor passively participate, it's now on us to dismantle it. It was built on our watch and it needs to burn on our watch.

When a platform we designed and built to connect people across the world is used to doxx the parents of murdered children, and the people who run it refuse to do anything about it; when they refuse to fix it because they don't see it as a problem; when they attempt to justify the profits with which they're lining their pockets as values, we need to burn it to the ground.

When the platform we use to talk to family and old friends turns into a gun marketplace, and the people who run it refuse to fix it, we need to burn it to the ground. When that same network moves so fast that they break not just things, but tender things, fragile things, things with names, for the sake of those names, we need to burn it to the ground.

When we refuse to let our own children use the fruits of our labor while still cashing the checks we're earning by addicting other people's children—all the while rending our garments over "what's happening to kids today!"—we need to burn all our work down. Nothing is *happening* to the children. We are *doing something* to the children.

When the sun crosses the Earth, it collects our stories along the way. Tales of outrage, aggression, marginalization, and exclusion. Tales of toxic masculinity and racism. Tales of teenagers being abused online to the point of suicide. Tales of women being harassed and threatened with unthinkable things. Tales of immigrants being abducted while they drop their children off at school. Tales about the tools we built with our own hands and enabled. That same sun eventually sets on Silicon Valley, a big flaming orange ball dropping into the ocean at the end of America, at the end of capitalism. Let the fires we set rival the orange glow of that setting sun. Let it all burn down.

Let those that come after us sift through the ashes to learn from our mistakes.

PART THREE

You Can't Go It Alone

Hold on, don't fight your war alone

Hate all around you, don't have to face it on
 your own

We will win this fight

Let all souls be brave

— Janelle Monáe

I promised you a hopeful book, and I meant that. That said, I now have to tell you that if you were hoping for a solution to the current mess in tech and design at the end of this book, you won't find one. I don't have a solution. If *any* white man told you they had a solution, I'd encourage you to run in the opposite direction as fast as you could. But, I do know this: by ourselves, we don't stand a chance. I can't solve it. You can't solve it. If we band together, we have a chance. If we properly define who we include in that *we*, then we might just have a *fighting* chance.

We have to see ourselves as being liable for our actions. We have to hold ourselves accountable for those actions, and just as importantly, our inactions. We need to hold our entire community accountable for doing the job the right way. We can and should argue. We can and should cajole. We can and should fight for the right thing. We can and should attempt to influence, educate, and instruct. And should those things fail...

Throwing ourselves on the gears is always an option. It takes bravery, but to deny the liability of our work means passing it on to the people who come in contact with it. We can't ask the people we're protecting to be braver than we're willing to be.

Finally, not doing the job correctly should have a cost. A doctor who steps outside their ethical framework loses the ability to practice medicine. A lawyer who steps outside their ethical framework loses the ability to practice law. A designer who builds a tool to lie to a regulatory body is likely to get a promotion. Time to end that bullshit.

A license, in and of itself, won't solve the problem, but like the other items on this list, it'll help. Ultimately, designers want to design. The idea that we could lose the ability to earn a living doing what we love by doing it wrong ends up being a strong motivation for doing it well. There are carrots and there are sticks. This is a necessary stick. Also, we had a chance to do the right thing within an unlicensed profession. We failed. Think of a license as those signs you see on heavy machinery telling you where not to stick your hands or your hair. They exist because some idiot stuck his hand in there. Doctors and lawyers need to be licensed because, well, someone stuck their hand in there. Now our hand is in there, too. Licensing for our profession is coming. This isn't necessarily a decision we'll have to make, as much as one which we'll have to prepare for.

In the next three chapters, we talk about the importance of community, professional organizations, and licensing. I believe these three things are instrumental to fixing the problem we've created. (Along with education, which we've already talked about.) Please consider these chapters the beginning of a discussion, a discussion I encourage you to continue with those around you.

The Case for Community

A few years ago, I gave a talk on the Facebook campus. Campus is the most important word in that sentence.

Corporations don't have offices anymore. They have campuses. That's not an accident. The last time *I* was part of a campus, I was in college. I have fond memories of that campus. I grew up there. I met my friends there. I ate there. I saw bands there. I fell in love there. I had my heart broken there and vice versa. I worked there. I shopped at the campus store. I even managed to attend a few classes there. For the first year of my college life, I lived there. For the length of my college stay, that campus was the center of my community. For people who attend college, this is the first community we experience outside the community in which we grew up. It's our first community as supposed adults, where we have a higher degree of agency.

"We're hardwired for community. We've been living in communities forever in terms of needing the numbers to go hunt or to go collect berries," says Dan Sinker. Dan has been building communities from the time he started *Punk Planet*, a magazine I probably read on that college campus, to his days running *Open News*, a community of news nerds. As Dan suggests, communities keep us safe. They protect us from elements outside the community. They allow us to share resources, and they provide us with an identity. This is why so many people return to those college campuses throughout their lives, hoping to rekindle that feeling of belonging.

Throughout our lives, we continue looking for communities where we can belong. For some of us, it's our neighborhood or another group of people with whom we share a common interest. For me, there are all the neighbors at the dog park whose names I don't even know, but I can give you a full rundown of their dogs' dietary restrictions. A community can be a group of people with whom we share a spiritual connection, such as in a church, synagogue, mosque, or Run the Jewels show. Sometimes community is thrust on us. People marching for a cause are a temporary community. We have a sense of belonging together. In all these cases, these are our people. We look out for each other and we keep each other safe.

As I walked through the Facebook campus, it reignited some of those same feelings from my college campus. There were shops, giant lawns, a climbing wall. (My state school did not have a climbing wall). There were people doing things that looked more like hanging out than doing work, and people were wearing clothes with the name of the company on it, just like on college campuses. (Picture John Belushi in the infamous COLLEGE sweatshirt from *Animal House*, except it says COMPANY.) Just as I went to school to supposedly go to class, these people were here to supposedly do work. Yet, the setting provided for so much more than that. It was obviously a community.

This is by design. Facebook and companies like Facebook want you to feel like you're not just at work, they want to be your de facto community. They'll provide you with everything you need. Not just a job, but also food, clothing, services to wash that clothing, social events, haircuts, gyms, health care, your favorite bands to play at events, and even on-campus mental health services (which raises so many red flags that it's beyond anything I can joke about). Modern tech campuses don't just rival college campuses, they obliterate them in scope, activities, and money. Losing a job doesn't just mean losing a paycheck, it means being ostracized from your community and, at least in Facebook's case, potentially losing access to your therapist! They're company towns. (Watch Matewan, kids. Know your history!)

There are communities which emerge organically, often without leaders—Occupy comes to mind—and communities which are purposely designed to be communities, such as college campuses and these new tech company towns. When something is designed, we need to look at the motives of the designer. Tech campuses are designed, first of all, to lure you in. (Not much different than a college campus, to be honest.) You interview. You visit the campus. It plays a role in which job you choose. Secondly, they're designed to keep you there. (Here we diverge from college campuses, which are happy to kick you out after four years to groom a new crop of future alumni dues targets.) They cater to your needs and whims. They provide sustenance. They provide necessary services. Thirdly, and most insidiously, they're designed to inspire loyalty, especially when the community is under attack. They may appear to be designed for the benefit of the worker, but the feelings of loyalty that the community is designed to engender benefit the company much, much more.

After the Facebook opposition research scandal broke, I reached out to a few Facebook employees. (They'll remain anonymous for obvious reasons.) While their initial reactions went from pretending this wasn't happening to being outraged and wanting to leave the company, within days they'd circled the wagons. Their collective mindset turned to something like "We'll be fine. We'll get through this." They were rallying in support of what they saw as their community, and by the insidious design of that community, they ended up protecting the corporation that designed it.

There's a dark side of communities as well. That dark side is insulation. When the reason for community changes from "keeping those inside safe" to "keeping those outside, out" we lose perspective. We stagnate, and we stop introducing new ideas. (Not to mention that this cripples the community's genetic pool.) We circle the wagons.

Where most of the world saw a story about corporate malfeasance and corruption, Facebook employees saw a story about their community being attacked and protecting itself. They circled the wagons. Their community was under attack. If your community was under attack, you'd circle the wagons, too. That's the problem. Their sense of community, as designed by the corporation, was stronger than their sense of loyalty to any community outside the company. (The benefits of being in that community are so immense!) It became easier to rally against outside forces than to question their community, not to mention their own complicity.

Many of those same Facebook employees will end their day by getting on luxury buses and riding up Highway 101 to San Francisco, a city where they sleep, eat brunch, and drink. Many of them don't view the city as their community. That's the problem. The tech bubble, which eviscerated the rental market and led to thousands of evictions within the city, didn't just destroy multiple communities. It replaced them with non-communities. San Francisco, once a vibrant imperfect city with a million weird and wonderful communities, has become a bedroom community for Silicon Valley. A huge swath of people working here don't see themselves as part of any community in the city. Their community is elsewhere and it was designed by their bosses.

If designers and other tech workers want to have any chance at fixing the mess we've created, we need to reassess who we consider our community. The homeless people whose existence we condemn in our Medium thinkpieces because they dare to exist close to the homes we pay too much rent for? *They* are our community. It would serve us all well to understand how we are failing them. The multitudes that get harassed and abused online by the very tools we build? *They* are our community. They deserve our allegiance. The corner bodega that's barely getting by because all their customers have been evicted? *They* deserve our business. The school system that's suffering because teachers can no longer afford to live where they teach? *They* deserve our tax money.

Now, is it possible for real community to exist within the Disneyfied campuses created by corporations? I wouldn't be asking the theoretical question if the answer was no. Obviously, it can. Communities can emerge anywhere. They can emerge wherever people have common goals. Whether it's getting everyone on our block to rake their leaves in the fall, cheering our local team, or marching for a cause. We saw this in the 2018 Google employee walkout. Google has many beautiful campuses across the world and I guarantee you they weren't designed so that workers can organize. Yet they did. Those workers ended up creating a real community within the one a corporation designed for them.

The people who would sack you in a heartbeat to improve their quarterly earnings report are not your community, and they don't deserve your allegiance. When companies design their workplaces to mimic the trappings of community (many tech workers go directly from college campuses to corporate campuses, making the mental mapping that much easier), they're taking all those good feelings that you have about community and transferring it to their own ends. They're buying your loyalty with corporate haircuts, weekend trips to Tahoe, and a therapist within walking distance of your desk—in an office where your manager can see who walks in and out.

One of the reasons humans band together in larger communities is to protect each other from something larger than ourselves. Our power derives from our collective power. We can't design things for the common good if the sole community we're representing is our boss. When we look out at a team with twelve people in it, we need to know that team is representing the best interests of twelve different communities. We need to know that team is doing something those communities need. We need to know that team is making sure that tool isn't going to have adverse effects on those communities. Will that slow us down? You bet. That's a feature, not a bug. We've seen where moving fast and breaking things has gotten us.

OUR STRENGTH IS IN OUR NUMBERS

On November 1, 2018, I was teaching an ethics workshop in Ottawa, Canada. One of the topics we covered that day was the power of organized protest. If you walk out of your job in protest, *you* have a problem. If you can talk your entire department into walking out with you, then *your company* has a problem. It's hard to replace an entire department, especially once people start asking why you're hiring an entire new department. Collectively, we have always had more power than we do individually. The attendees at the workshop might've been buying all of this in theory. But practically, who's going to do that? Who walks out on their job anymore?

As the workshop drew to a close, I tried to content myself with the fact that I'd gotten people maybe halfway there. Then I glanced at my phone and saw an alert about 22,000 employees world-wide walking out of their jobs at Google to protest the company's mishandling of a high-profile sexual harassment case.[38] It was happening. The world noticed. The workshop attendees who were all packing up to leave noticed. They were all looking at the same, or similar, alerts. They looked at each other. They looked back at me and I saw hope in their eyes. What I'd (maybe) convinced them to be true in theory, they were now seeing as possible in practice. 22,000 employees at one of the biggest, most powerful companies in the world, across multiple time zones, had organized. They communicated. They planned. They made an impact. The story wasn't reported as being about disgruntled employees, which it might have had there been three or four employees standing outside a building. It was reported as being about bad corporate policy, which it very much was. Sexual harassment, to be exact.

When *we* organize, *they* have a problem. Even the biggest companies in the world are made up of people like *us*.

As we discussed in the last chapter, one of the questions we need to ask ourselves is where the line is. What's the thing that makes you put down the tools? 22,000 Google employees showed us where the line was for them. That walkout brought attention to a situation, and it told the company they'd crossed a line, a line those employees wouldn't cross with them.

On November, 14, 2018, *The New York Times* published a story on how Facebook dealt with the combined crises of Russian meddling, data hacking, and hate speech. This is the paragraph that caught my eye:

Facebook employed a Republican opposition-research firm to discredit activist protesters, in part by linking them to the liberal financier George Soros. It also tapped its business relationships, persuading a Jewish civil rights group to cast some criticism of the company as anti-Semitic.

Facebook hired a firm to paint one of their critics as being anti-Semitic. Sadly, it wasn't Facebook's behavior that surprised me. A scorpion does what a scorpion knows how to do. What surprises me is that Facebook employees are still at their desks after finding that their company was actively attempting to discredit a critic in such a foul method. No doubt some of them are shook. No doubt some of them will make public statements against their company's policy, and those are needed. No doubt there will be internal spirited conversations within the company, and those are needed as well, but there won't be a walk-out. I wrote this hours after the article was released. I doubted I would have to come back to this paragraph and revise it and that was sadly true.

Facebook employees, with a few individual exceptions, don't believe their company has crossed a line yet. Twitter employees, again with a few individual exceptions, don't believe their company has crossed a line yet. We know this because they haven't put down the tools. By continuing to aid the companies making those decisions by selling them their labor, they've become complicit in their actions. They haven't organized. They haven't made a stand.

And they won't.

Believe it or not, that's the hopeful part. Companies where employees aren't taking a stand, companies where employees aren't awake to the complicity of their labor, companies where employees aren't willing to put the tools down and take an ethical stand, will eventually die. They're creating a workforce no one wants to join, and building toxic products no one wants to use. Their short-term decisions are digging their long-term resting place. After watching 22,000 Google employees walk out in protest of their company's unethical actions, I know someone's watching the gate. I'm more inclined to trust them. Not necessarily because I trust the company, but because the employees have shown me that I can trust *them*.

Our only way out of this mess is to work together.

We need to see ourselves as a community, and not just a community of common interests, but a community of common agency. We're a workforce. The way one of us works ends up affecting all of us. As long as one of us is willing to work as a pair of hands, there's someone out there you can hire to be a pair of hands. If we agree that we work within an ethical framework, as most other professions of our caliber do, then we can elevate not just the type of work we do and how we do it, but also the society which that work ends up affecting. Imagine what a different world we'd be living in today if Twitter employees had reacted to hatred, abuse, and harassment on their platform by demanding change, and putting down their tools until they were heard. That world was within our reach. If Twitter employees had the courage to walk out, the world would be a different place today.

According to *The Intelligencer's* Brian Feldman[39], Mark Zuckerberg gathered his staff together shortly after the Facebook opposition scandal broke and described the story as "bullshit." *(Narrator: It's not. The New York Times has the receipts.)* Zuckerberg is responsible for at least two communities: the community of people who use his service and the community that builds it. He betrayed the former a long time ago, and I can't be absolutely certain of exactly when he betrayed the latter, but lying to his own workers is definitely on the short list of candidates.

IS IT TOO LATE TO START A DESIGN COMMUNITY?

Along with the communities where we live, socialize, and learn, it's of utmost importance to understand that we're a professional community as well. We're a group of people brought together because we share a craft and solve the same family of problems, and I don't mean the monthly meetup that's actually a thinly-veiled recruitment gathering for the company hosting the event.

I asked Matt Haughey, who started the long-running and popular community site *Metafilter*, if it was too late to start a design community. Here's his reply:

> "No, I don't think it's ever too late to start anything. I mean, the world's not done being formed in any aspect. So I can think of anything as the most established subject matter in the world and still think someone new can come along and just do it anytime they like, and do a better job of it and offer someone a different way. It wouldn't be easy, but it's possible."

We can do this.

The Case for Professional Organizations

One of the first things I did when I got my first real design paycheck was to join the *American Institute of Graphic Arts* or AIGA.

(For those outside the United States, your country probably has a local version. For example, in Australia it's the AGDA.) Joining felt like a big deal, like I was making the decision that I was serious about this design thing, and willing to tithe part of my salary to a professional organization. As a student, the AIGA was held up as an organization to which we should aspire to be a member. All our teachers were members. The dead designers we looked up to had all been members. The living designers we looked up to were all members. I was excited to be a member as well. As human beings, we yearn to find our people and I'd been told these were my people. At the time, it was the premier professional organization for designers. Some would argue it still is, although I'm no longer one of them.

After joining, I waited by the mailbox and I wasn't disappointed. AIGA mail came on an almost constant basis. It was the most well-designed mail I'd ever gotten! From the paper stock to the printing methods to the visuals themselves, it was impeccable. Beautiful postcards. Beautiful booklets. Beautiful posters. So many beautiful posters. I hung many of them up. With every new poster came the call for a poster contest to provide the next round of posters.

There came a point, as I was accumulating all of this printed matter that I started asking myself, well, what does the AIGA actually *do* for me other than being inspirational? As a new designer trying to keep his neck above water, I was looking for advice on how to do the job, how to get paid, how to make ends meet, how to deal with clients and bosses, difficult workplace situations, etc. You know, things that would actually help me generate the cost of next year's membership. I wasn't finding much of that.

As I transitioned from graphic design to what at the time was still called web design, I started wondering how much of what the AIGA was doing even applied to me. I was still a designer—I still cared about all the stuff designers cared about—but the AIGA seemed to behave as if the web didn't exist, much less employ designers. Did the AIGA care about people like me?

I would get my answer about twenty years later.

In 2016, I was invited to speak at the AIGA's annual gathering in Las Vegas and truthfully, I was honored to be there. I gave a twenty-minute talk about how designers needed a professional organization that had our backs so that we could work as ethically as possible. I wanted to know that if designers at Facebook, for example, were fearing retribution against pushing back, there'd be an organization that we could call for backup. I remember saying they should take the money they use for poster contests to hire lawyers. It got a big laugh from the audience. (It's always nice to get a laugh.) As an example of an organization that looks after its members, I brought up the AARP (The American Association for Retired People), which not only organizes group discounts on services retired people need, but keeps an army of lawyers in the air at all times in case someone refuses to give an old person an early bird discount.

The talk went well, and I retired to the couch in the green room to catch my breath. As I sat there, a well known designer, who's part of the

AIGA brass and someone I'd looked up to my whole professional life, sat down next to me and said, "That was a good talk," which made me feel good. The next part didn't. They followed it up by telling me that although it was a good talk, it didn't have anything to do with design because what we did out there in Silicon Valley wasn't really design.

So it goes. I'd gone to Las Vegas to find out if the AIGA could still be the professional organization we needed, and I had my answer. It could not, because it wasn't interested in doing so.

Like Blockbuster Video, who eroded into oblivion because they didn't anticipate the importance of streaming video, the AIGA dug their own grave of irrelevance by ignoring UX designers that were part of their community.

The AIGA's position on designers who work on the web has been to ignore them, possibly hoping that they'd go away or start their own thing, which *kind* of happened. The IxDA was started in 2005 to serve the needs of interaction designers. Unfortunately, they saw this as a separate field from visual designers, the field purportedly served by the AIGA. In short, the AIGA saw web designers as tech people, and the IxDA saw us as graphics people, and we fell through the cracks of two organizations that had put too narrow a definition on design.

Let me tell you one of my old client services tricks from way back. One of the very first things I'd do as soon as I had access to the client team was to search out their designer. There was usually one, sometimes two, but not often. Sadly, they'd usually been left off the project I'd been brought in to do, even though they were indispensable to the project's success. My goal was to get them on the project. When I found them, it was like a scene where someone thinks they're the last of a species and suddenly there's another and they're no longer alone. These kids had been treated so badly by their bosses that once I reached out to them and extended a hand in friendship, they'd tell me alllllll the company dirt. That's how starved designers were to meet other people like them. As designers were headed off to try their hand at unexplored mediums, the professional services that were supposed to be watching out for them had turned their backs.

For better or worse, professional organizations are incredibly important to a community. Setting standards. Resolving disputes. Collective organizing. Codes of professional conduct. They are the optimal recourse to things like legal representation, group insurance for self-employed, and even financial services. Not to mention the sense of confidence that comes from collective empowerment. Many of the designers I know from the early days of the web, and even a few today, can tell you stories about being the only designer in the room. One designer among hundreds of engineers, fresh out of school with no role models, no mentors in sight, and no professional organization to lean on.

If you think I'm calling for the unionization of designers, you'd be right. A professional organization is by any other name a union, so let's stop beating around the bush. We need a union. In fact, my first book, *Design Is a Job*, contained a line about designers needing a union. It was edited out, and I didn't fight to keep it in. That was in 2012. The world was a simpler place, we were still naive about what a true cesspool we were in the middle of building. I wonder if I would've fought harder to keep it in knowing where we were headed as an industry.

My dad spent the majority of his life as a construction worker in Pennsylvania, which freezes over in the winter. Every year, as the ground started to freeze over, whatever company he was working for would lay him off. Yet, we never went hungry because every couple of weeks, someone from the union would show up with groceries, call my mom ma'am, tousle my hair, and have a beer on the porch with my dad. It wasn't the company doing that. It was the union. So yeah, I have a soft spot for them. No one knows the plight of a worker better than another worker. When one worker is in trouble, I've seen other workers give the shirts off their backs to help out.

Collectively, we are amazing. Collectively, every weakness one of us has is another's strength. Don't be a cog in *their* machine. Not when we can use all those cogs to build our *own* machine!

A WELL-RUN PROFESSIONAL ORGANIZATION

Aren't unions filled with unethical mobsters on the take? Some, sure. Anytime you get people together, the possibility they'll behave badly is on the table. That goes for unions, governments, corporations, and PTAs. Corruption certainly isn't exclusive to unions. The idea that Silicon Valley corporate management would throw shade at anyone else for being corrupt is comedic, but let's not throw the baby out with the bathwater. There's another possibility: sometimes when people get together they can actually make something amazing.

By definition, unions are a collection of workers who share a common goal, resources, and who act in a collective interest. As the saying goes, if organizing workers were so ineffective, why would so many companies work so hard to keep you from doing it?

It's worth discussing how I believe a professional organization for designers would operate. To do that, all I have to do is look back to what I was expecting the AIGA to be when I first joined, and marry it with what I've learned from being in this business for over twenty years. Plus, I already gave you the list above, so let's just flesh it out:

ORIENTATION TO THE PROFESSION

School teaches you how to be good at school. I don't care what design school you went to, it didn't teach you how to do the job. Everything you learned in school can be undone by one shitty client or one shitty boss that you're not prepared for. A professional organization can prepare you for how to work because its membership is comprised of people who are doing the work, at every level. It's filled with workers. If you want to learn how to work, there's no better teacher than another worker. You'd meet people who've been in the business for decades, as well as people who'd shown up just a few years before you. You could learn from each other. These people could help you get your first job because they'd work at places that were hiring. They could counsel you on the right place for you to work, as well as the ones to avoid.

SETTING STANDARDS

Working for free. Spec work. "This'll be good for your portfolio." Being handed a new project on Friday afternoon and being expected to finish it by Monday. Being expected to answer email or take calls on the weekend. Expanding scope on a project without earning more or even getting more time. And obviously, the worst of the bunch, doing work you know is ethically unsound. I have done every one of these things! I'm guessing you've done a few yourself. The reason I did them was because I was never taught not to!

I was never taught that pushing back was an option. In fact, in school, we were taught to bring clients gifts! Gifts! Way to cement a power dynamic. Professionals do not hand you gifts. They are hired to solve a problem they are experts in solving. They solve it, and they hand you an invoice.

As mentioned, when I talk to designers about working ethically and responsibly, the response I get most often is, "they'll just get someone else to do it," which, to be clear, is a shitty reason to do anything. I wish everyone who thought that way would quit the business, but what if we took even *that* shitty response away? What if we worked together to establish a set of professional standards, so that every designer was working from a common set of rules? None of us works for free. None of us does spec work. We can all be empowered to say, "no," because we know that every other designer would line up behind us.

A common set of standards is the first step to acting collectively and harnessing our power. Is this hard to do? Of course, but since every other profession worth their salt has figured this out, we also know it's not impossible.

COLLECTIVE ORGANIZING

On November 1, 2018, two very important events happened. First, 22,000 Google employees staged a walkout over unfair labor practices. I mentioned this in the previous chapter. The second event is related to the first. Across Silicon Valley, that walkout resulted in the collective sphincter tightening of every CEO and venture capitalist in tech. It was a glorious sound, like the sound of a giant boiled egg getting sucked into a glass bottle, doubtlessly with an odor to match.

That walkout scared the shit out of management across the board because if Google employees could organize and walk out, their employees could do the same. Imagine Twitter employees crowding the pavement of San Francisco's Market street demanding that management take user harassment seriously. Imagine Facebook employees gathered onto their fancy campus demanding that Facebook do something about protecting user data. I have no doubt that a lot of sleep was lost that night. They didn't have to worry, though.

No one else organized. Again, I know there are workers inside both these companies that want to do the right thing. I know both those companies have lost a lot of talent because workers were uncomfortable with the work they were being asked to do, as well as the work they weren't being allowed to do. Clearly, the desire is there so why didn't the Google walkout have a bigger ripple effect?

Some of this is answered in the previous chapter. Workers feel a closer community connection to a company that provides for all their needs than they do to the communities they actually live in, but it goes beyond that. It's the fear of losing that community; fear of losing the amenities that come with it, and understandably, fear of losing their livelihood. So, they either drink the Kool-Aid and convince themselves they're doing more good inside than out. (This is only true if you're actually *doing* something. Last I checked collecting a paycheck and going on quarterly team trips to Tahoe wasn't an act of resistance.) Or else they find another job so they can leave without missing a paycheck—rent is real. But there's a third option and the third option is the ethical and responsible option. That option is to organize. If the company you're working at is doing unethical work, and you've tried every option to convince them to stop, putting down the tools is the most ethical, responsible option open to you.

To organize you need an organization.

In her spectacular book, *Twitter and Tear Gas* (which I'd encourage you all to read), Zeynep Tufekci makes the case that one of the reasons the so-called Twitter revolutions in Turkey and Egypt failed was because they lacked the planning infrastructure of the Civil Rights Movement of the 1960s, which had to move slowly and deliberately. They didn't have Twitter. You couldn't tweet out tomorrow's protest. It had to make the rounds, phone trees, whisper and sneaker nets. What they lacked in speed and immediacy, they made up in depth and organization. A professional organization for designers—and I'll remind you one more time that you're *all* designers—would give us that organization. While the idea of Norma Rae jumping on her desk and staging a walkout is fierce and romantic, most labor actions happen slowly and deliberately.

If you're sitting there saying, "we don't wanna move slowly and deliberately," well... apart from those people at Google and a team at Microsoft who rallied against their face recognition software being used by ICE, you ain't exactly been moving quickly, either.

RESOLVING DISPUTES

A few months ago, a very good friend of mine found out the recruiter who'd hired her into a company had lied about her pay scale. She'd been told she was coming in at the highest pay scale possible for her position. Instead, she'd come in at the lowest. She checked around with others in her department and found out this was happening to women across the department. The recruiter was giving different information to male and female recruits. She took this information to her manager. Things got weird. Performance reviews, which had been stellar to that point, started going badly and getting strangely personal. My friend, who'd been very much enjoying working at this company and, from what I could see, doing a bang-up job, started looking for work somewhere else. She'd been labeled a troublemaker.

Systematic problems like that need to be handled by an organization equal to the workplace with the problem, not by the individual affected by the problem. In this particular situation, that individual was acting on be-half of several people. My friend's performance reviews didn't start going badly because she was performing her job badly, they started going badly because she was pointing out a systematic issue *outside* of her job duties.

Imagine having an organization of our own to handle this shit. Imagine spending our time at work being able to do the job we were hired to do—the job we will ultimately be judged on at those performance reviews.

LEGAL REPRESENTATION

About two years into running our own studio, we got into a messy sit-uation with a bad client. He threatened to sue us, and we were terrified. I started catastrophizing all of these situations where we'd end up in court, lose all our money, our studio, and end up in jail. Obviously, this was over-the-top but the fear was real, and I was a nervous wreck. We eventually made a few phone calls and got referred to a young lawyer who was just starting out in his career. We called him up, made an appointment, and met face-to-face. We told him about the client threatening to sue us and he said the most magical thing I've ever heard.

"This sounds like bullshit. Want me to make it go away?"

He called the shitty client, informed him he was our lawyer, and that was that. We never heard from the client again. The lawyer, however, is with us to this day. If you do a Google search for my name and "fuck you pay me," you can meet him. His name's Gabe Levine.

That client was intimidating us. He was counting on us to be scared, and we were. My partner and I felt like it was just the two of us against him and the entire justice system. He was taking advantage of us. Like any standard run-of-the-mill bully, once he saw that we had our own legal backup, he ran off. Now, imagine this at a professional scale. I believe there are designers out there trying to work responsibly and ethically. (I have to believe that. The alternative is too scary.) When those designers attempt to do the job the right way, they get bullied, they get intimidated, or it just feels like they're alone. Legal representation from a professional organization would mean never feeling alone again.

It would mean that any designer harassed or fired for doing their job correctly wouldn't have to go hunting for a lawyer because one would be provided. Even better, the odds that you would be harassed or fired would decrease substantially because you would know you aren't alone.

This is probably a good place to talk about your human resources department. In February of 2017, Susan Fowler published a brave and extensive essay of her tenure at Uber. It eventually led to the ousting of CEO Travis Kalanick, a walking roofie. In that essay, she detailed the many many incidents of harassment she encountered at the company and how her human resources department refused to do anything about them. Your human resources department does not work for you. They work for your employer. Their job is to protect them, not you. They're the department of Judas. (Not to say there aren't decent people in HR departments. There are. I've met some, but they are few and far between.) Legal representation from your professional organization would work for you and be paid through your professional dues.

GROUP BENEFITS

According to a study published October 22, 2018, 57.3 million Americans are freelance workers, or in today's parlance, gig workers. This includes contractors, people hired for a specific job, or for a specific amount of time. As a cost-saving measure, workers with higher paying jobs are more likely to be contracted than hired. In tech, the numbers are higher. According to the same report, in 2018, Google contract workers started outnumbering employees. Companies like Uber, who's whole proposition involves a need for drivers, won't even acknowledge those workers as part of their workforce.

The vast majority of these people receive no benefits from their employers. That means they don't have medical, dental, or vision insurance. (My Scandinavian and Canadian readers just passed out again, bless them.) That means a health issue becomes a financial crisis. That means dependents don't have access to care unless there's another parent who's lucky enough to have a job with benefits. That means kids with bad vision aren't being tested, so they're falling behind in school because they can't see. This isn't even getting into things like life insurance and 401(k) savings plans. This is life without a safety net.

Tech companies do this for a simple reason—benefits are expensive; they want to maximize profits; and they're cheap. Gig workers have two main options: go without insurance or buy their own. (Two days before writing this, a federal judge in the US ruled that Obamacare was illegal. It's once again headed to the Supreme Court, where Brett "I like beer!" Kavanaugh will get to decide if you can get affordable health care.)

Obviously, this wouldn't be a problem if the United States offered Medicare-for-all. While I believe that may happen one day, it's not happening soon enough. A professional organization would have the power and finances to purchase insurance from a provider in bulk and to offer it to its members at a lower price than the members could purchase for themselves. Will it be difficult? Extremely. Time consuming? Almost guaranteed. Impossible? No. Other organizations have managed to pull this off. The Screen Actors Guild, for example, offers health insurance to qualifying members. The OPEIU, which represents the workers of SFMOMA, offers their members life insurance, student debt reduction programs, and scholarships. UNITE HERE, which represents hotel workers, offers legal assistance to immigrant workers whose work authorization changes. This could be of interest to designers here on H1-B visas, who might hesitate to do the right thing because they fear not just losing their job, but being deported. These are just a few examples. Unions, guilds, and other professional organizations have been leveraging their membership numbers to get bulk discounts on benefits forever. We should do the same.

FINANCIAL SERVICES

Okay, we're obviously into stretch goals now, but screw it. What's the point of rising up if we're not also rising up to control our own finances? Imagine banking at a credit union that's catered specifically for designers. Teachers do it. Firefighters do it. There's a proud tradition of credit unions all over the world. Member-owned, and in line with the needs of their members. Although technically a bank (the difference being that at a credit union, members are owners, kinda like a co-op), the USAA has been providing financial services for veterans and their families since 1922. I know a few people who use them and they swear by them. There are models out there for how to do this. It's not impossible.

Writer John Steinbeck once noted that American workers tend to see themselves as "temporarily embarrassed millionaires." Nowhere is this more true than in the rat king palaces of Silicon Valley. We don't think much about workers' rights because no one plans on being a worker for too long. I've personally had people complain to me that they hadn't made their first million by age thirty-five. We see work as a way to pass the time during our vesting schedules, so we're happy to trade away those rights for things that'll matter once we get over the fence.

Many of our ancestors fought, and I don't mean metaphorically, for decent working conditions, fair pay, benefits, decent working hours, time off, and the right to bargain collectively. Some of our ancestors even died to give us these things. I'm not exaggerating. It's because of them that we have weekends off, the eight-hour day, and paid overtime. Except you just read that sentence and realized that you don't have those things anymore, didn't you?

We don't get to make fun of poor people buying lottery tickets or poor people voting against their self-interests when we've traded all our hard-won worker's rights for stock options, a campus masseuse, and swordfish at the company cafeteria on Fridays.

The Case for Licensing & Regulation

Shortly after my eighteenth birthday, I got my driver's license.

To do this, I had to pass two tests: a written test and a driving test. Theory and practice. I had to study for both. This was pre-internet, so my Dad and I went to the Department of Motor Vehicles in Philadelphia and picked up a learner's permit and a test guide to study for the written part. (For the record, this was the *only* time I've ever been to the DMV where I thought, "I can't wait to come back here!") Over the next couple of months, I spent my evenings reading through the test manual trying to memorize all the rules of the road, what different signals meant, and how to deal with other drivers who were sharing the road with me. That part was pretty easy. On the weekends, my dad would drive me to an empty parking lot and we'd practice parking, three-point turns, signaling, braking, and not killing each other. He also taught me basic engine maintenance like how to change the oil, replace the air filter, and check transmission fluid. (Also, for the record, I learned to drive in a '79 Plymouth Volaré station wagon. It was harvest gold with fake wood paneling. Once I got my license, my dad handed me the keys, which I later realized was his way of avoiding having the talk about sex because that car was a purity pledge on wheels.) After a couple of months of practice, my dad decided I was ready to head back to the DMV and take my tests. If memory serves, I did pretty well on the written test, not as well—but enough to pass—on the driving test, and I got my license.

Every society around the world has decided we need a driver's license before we get behind the wheel of a motor vehicle. We treat getting a driver's license as a rite of passage. In fact, in most places, a driver's license is your primary form of legal identification. (In the United States, someone who doesn't want to learn to drive still has to go to the DMV and get a non-driving identification card, which are pretty common with people who grow up in big cities and manage to get around using public transportation.) We understand how dangerous driving can be, so we regulate cars in order to make them safer, and we license drivers in order to make sure they know the basics. Does this ensure the roads are safe? Absolutely not. They're crazy dangerous and far too many people still die in cars or in car-related ways every day. Imagine how much worse it would be if we didn't regulate vehicles and license drivers. I wouldn't get on that road. The body count would be much higher.

It took about twenty years for driver's licenses to become a thing and it was gradual. The first modern car was patented in 1886 by Karl Benz. (It was—as you may have guessed—a Benz. Dudes love naming things after themselves.) The first driver's licenses in the US were issued in 1903 by Massachusetts and Missouri. You didn't need to pass an exam to get them. California didn't start issuing licenses until 1913, and didn't require exams until 1927. For the first couple of decades of cars' existence, they were a curiosity that shared the road with carriages, horses, and scared the occasional cow. They operated on roads that were intended for much different traffic. Once their numbers rose, and they started crashing into each other and into other things, we started regulating them.

When people start dying, we regulate industries and we license practitioners.

We understand there are things in the world that are inherently dangerous. We understand that those things require a set of knowledge and skills to operate. Let's stick with the motor vehicles metaphor awhile longer. Long after I'd ridden the Volaré into the ground, I decided to get a scooter. (It was a phase. Like that week you decided you looked good in a fedora.) This involved going back to the DMV, and taking a different test to get a different type of license. In this particular case, the test involved a lot of stuff about defensive maneuvers because I'd be a smaller vehicle on the road. If my life had gone differently, I might've decided to become a long haul driver or a bus driver, both of which require unique license types and unique tests. Society doesn't want you behind the wheel of a bus unless you can prove you know what you're doing behind the wheel of a bus. Again, this doesn't eliminate bus accidents, but imagine being on the road and finding yourself surrounded by a bunch of buses being driven by people who don't know how to drive a bus. It's more than a little terrifying.

Licensing and regulation rarely eliminate a problem, but they do minimize it, and add accountability to the equation.

Getting a driver's license is a slight pain in the ass. It takes time and it costs money. In some places, you have to take a driving class before you can even take the test. You don't even get a good photo out of it! Yet, despite the current anti-regulation fervor in the United States, there's no movement to do away with driver's licenses or auto industry safety regulations, because we understand that driving is dangerous. We don't want to die in our cars. We don't want to get hit by cars, and we're okay with mostly anything that makes the road just a little bit safer.

Yet, the roads are still dangerous. In fact, it's safer to fly. No industry in the world is more regulated than the airline industry. From the mechanics who keep the planes in shape to the pilots who fly them to the traffic controllers who keep them from crashing into each other—the practitioners are licensed. Flight attendants deal with all manner of medical emergencies, as well as idiotic passenger behavior. They undergo a training program of ten or twelve weeks with written and practical exams before they can serve their first flight. According to my friend Erin, who was a flight attendant for three years, eighty percent of the training is about keeping passengers alive and the remaining twenty percent is about keeping passengers (reasonably) happy. Plus, there's recurring yearly training to make sure flight attendants are on top of their game, and are aware of any new regulations.

We've decided as a society that planes will not fall out of the sky. There's a couple of reasons for this. The first is hopefully obvious. When planes fall out of the sky, people die and we don't want that. The second is because a lot of people are still afraid of flying. In a recent study published in *Frontiers in Psychology*, forty percent of Americans self-diagnosed themselves as being afraid of flying. (Yeah, that number seems high to me too, but it's a self-diagnosis and, well, if someone thinks they're afraid of flying, the safe thing is to believe them.) The airline industry needs to do everything in its power to convince those forty percent that flying is really safe. Safety and regulation is the airline industry's most effective marketing campaign possible. We want to know that the people responsible for keeping us in the air are very, very good at keeping us in the air. They've taken tests! They have a license to do what they're doing. They wear quasi-military uniforms.

In fact, it's reassuring to have your captain greet you before the flight takes off. They sound calm. They sound professional. They've all adopted the Chuck Yeager accent. They call themselves not just a captain, but *your* captain, and they give you a weather update on the city to which you're headed. There is absolutely no reason for them to do this other than to reassure you that you'll get there. They're making you think of the destination rather than the journey.

Now imagine logging onto Facebook and hearing, "this is your captain, Mark Zuckerberg. I look forward to getting your content today. My sales team will be going through the cabin and siphoning off your data to the highest bidder."

I've been designing things online for over twenty years. Some of the things I've designed have been requests for people's personal data, including financial and medical information. I have absolutely no training to do this other than on-the-job training. Like most of the people who've been designing things online as long as I have, I just showed up and started doing things. Matt Haughey, who's been designing things online even longer than I have, put it this way: "we built up an industry around nothing, there was no history to it. We built the plane as we were flying it. My first job didn't require any technical degree because there wasn't one."

I'd say that people like me and Matt snuck in the side door, except we didn't. We just waltzed right through the front door because it was unlocked. We had no idea what we were doing back then. It was fun. It was exciting, and the stakes were much, much lower. We were like two fools racing their cars on a stretch of Nebraska dirt road without anyone else around. Had the internet stayed that size, we would've probably been safe doing that forever. But it didn't stay that size. Other people showed up, a lot more. We built more roads. We put in signals. Some idiot put up advertising, and now we have enough traffic—and we've had enough accidents—that it's time to make sure the roads are safe.

Okay, I've driven the car metaphor as far as I can.

I've been talking to designers about our craft being licensed for the past year in preparation for this book. The results have been as unanimous as they are negative. They don't want it. In fact, the replies run somewhere between "hell no" to taking a swing at me for even bringing it up. It's not a popular topic. I'll go into some of the reasoning I've heard against the idea in this chapter. To be absolutely fair, some of the concerns are legitimate, but here's the thing that gives me pause: when I ask the same people whether they'd go to an unlicensed doctor, they say no. When I ask them whether they'd fly with an unlicensed pilot, they say no. When I ask them whether they'd seek legal advice from an unlicensed lawyer, they say no. When we see ourselves as users of professional services, we want the reassurance of knowing that someone somewhere vouched for the person we're trusting. When we see ourselves as the professionals delivering those services, we believe people don't deserve that same reassurance we ourselves crave. That's hypocritical.

"But Mike, those other professions do dangerous things. They could get us killed!" Seriously? We're dealing with the data of most of the world. We're dealing with privacy concerns of the human beings. Elections have been hacked using tools we built. We have the CEO of Facebook saying that what's good for the world isn't necessarily what's good for Facebook. (He did.[40]) And yes, decisions we have *made* or *failed to make* have gotten people killed.

Throughout this book, I've mentioned Victor Papanek's *Design For the Real World*. I mentioned the first sentence of the book: "There are professions more harmful than industrial design, but only a few of them." Among the few that Papanek was referring to were industries like mining, the military, etc. User experience design didn't exist when that sentence was written, but it belongs there. The lapses in our professional judgment and skills have brought the world to the brink of disaster, or at the very least, given bad actors the avenue for doing so. What we do is dangerous. The way we've gone about doing it is reprehensible. We need to be reined in.

So, should designers be licensed? Well, the question is a red herring. Some of us already are. The aforementioned industrial designers are licensed to the gills. Some of us work in industries that are heavily regulated, so we're not unfamiliar with the process of being vetted to work in those industries. So, the real question is should user experience designers themselves be licensed? Since there's an argument to be made that the work we do is just as dangerous, if not more so, than our brothers and sisters in industrial design, I'd argue that the real question isn't whether user experience designers should be licensed, but when, and even more importantly—by whom?

There's a misconception that *we'll* be making the decision on whether designers should be licensed. That's probably not the case. More likely than not, that decision will be made for us by governing bodies at the state, national, or even international level. Licensing is a form of regulation, and regulation tends to happen when an industry is found guilty of not being able to regulate itself—of which we're more than guilty. In fact, we've been flaunting how little we want to regulate ourselves. (The goal, after all, was disruption. Goal achieved.) We're already seeing good regulation regarding privacy, such as the GDPR, which came out of the European Union (who are years ahead of the US on this stuff, like they were on accessibility). We're also seeing shit regulation like the destruction of net neutrality coming out of a US government that believes the internet is a series of tubes.

I don't claim to have all, or even many, of the answers to the licensing question. Of all the topics in this book, this is the one I feel the most conflicted about. This is a difficult topic, and I don't have the answers. I'm building an argument, not providing a solution. The solution needs to come from more than one person. It needs to come from us as a community. We're good at solving problems, and hopefully I've convinced you of one thing in this book—the more diverse points of view we throw at a problem, the stronger the solution will be.

Do I want it to be more difficult for you to be a designer? Yes and no. I want it to be more difficult for you to design some things. A restaurant license doesn't preclude you from cooking for your friends and family. It does, however, mean that you need prove you know a few things before you can start cooking for strangers coming in off the street and exchanging money to eat in your restaurant.

Do I care if you have a license before you design your friend's black metal band logo? No, I do not. Make it fierce. Do I care if you have a license before you design a website for your dad's construction company? No, I do not. Help your dad. Do I care if you have a license when you're designing data collection for two billion people? Yes, I do. Actually, it's not even the license that I care about. I care that you know what you're doing. I care that you understand the job and the ethics behind the job. I care that someone has tested you on this knowledge and you've passed those tests. The reason I care about those tests, those signifiers, is because I've seen us run up a body count. A license is a signifier that we're qualified to make decisions about the thing they're asking us to do. (Yes, we can wave that license in their face when they argue with us about the ethics of what they're asking for.) You cannot get upset or surprised when you've been working unethically and someone decides to slap a governor on you. We had an opportunity to work ungoverned, and we failed. When the people we work for are out there saying things like, "what's good for us isn't necessarily what's good for the world," I need to know that we're in place as a check on their idiocy.

Every industry starts out wild and then matures. The dangerous ones get regulated for society's safety. We need to care more about the safe-being of the people using what we design than we care about how much profit those things generate. The world needs us in place to keep monsters away.

THE ARGUMENTS AGAINST LICENSING

Who grants the licenses?

In 2018, California legalized weed. In the first quarter of 2018, the state of California granted over 5,000 licenses to growers, distributors, dispensaries, and manufacturers. (Half those licenses appear to be in a half-mile radius of my house.) The rollout didn't go off without a hitch. It sputtered. It stalled, and it had hiccups all over the place. By and large, it pretty much worked. This is amazing if you consider that the state was licensing an industry from scratch with no federal help whatsoever and making sure to handle tons of local variances. Different counties wanted different things. The state took that all into account. At the same time, it was dealing with the incredibly difficult problem of decriminalizing an industry. What do you do with people you've put in jail for doing the thing that's now legal? (To their credit, the city of Oakland issued fifty percent of their weed licenses to people who'd been arrested for selling weed in the last ten years, as reparations for the ridiculous and racist war on drugs.)

While the state of California was licensing all of these people and businesses, it was also figuring out how to regulate this whole mess. None of this was easy, but it's being done. It's not perfect, and I imagine a lot of change in the next few years as the newly-formed industry matures. Luckily, it had a good example to follow. Colorado legalized weed in 2012. So when California finally came to its senses, it was able to study what Colorado had done right and wrong. It had a template from which to at least start working.

So, when we ask who would grant licenses for designers, all we have to do is look to other skilled professionals. Who licenses them? I asked my lawyer, Gabe Levine. He got his license from the California State Bar Association. It's what you call a licensing body. Their board is made up of thirteen people. Seven of them are lawyers, and six of them are not. So, people who do what they do, and people who are affected by what they do. You have to pass the bar exam, and then you show up and they give you your license. They can also take it away if you do something dumb, like commit a crime or behave unethically. There's a group of people who are part of your community who give you a license to practice your craft and take it away if you do a shitty job.

Yeah, we can do this. Hard, but not impossible.

Licensing and regulation limits innovation

To believe this is to believe there is a lack of innovation in licensed fields. Can you seriously tell me there's no innovation in the medical field? Take a look at Dubai's skyline and tell me there's no innovation in architecture. Telecommunications is one of the most regulated fields on Earth. Anyone who remembers the sound of a 2400-baud modem knows we've come a long way. LED lights were invented because the government said we had to make our light bulbs more efficient. Obviously, the afore-mentioned auto industry has made significant innovation in getting away from fossil fuels in the last few decades, all under regulatory supervision.

If anything, regulations encourage innovation. They give us the con-straints we need around which to design solutions. Let's bring the con-versation back around to our own backyard for a bit. It wasn't too long ago that designers were arguing about having to make websites accessible. Thankfully, that fight is (almost) over. But holy shit, do I remember the wailing and the screaming (some of it, I'll admit, coming from my own mouth) because our almighty design vision was being screwed with. Didn't people realize we were auteurs?! People with physical disabilities limited our innovation of parallax scrolling by getting motion sickness. Colorblind people limit our innovation by having issues with our nuanced color palettes! Worst of all, poor people in remote areas limit our innovation by only having phones with spotty reception. Get some bandwidth, poor people! Yeah, we're terrible.

What I hear when designers complain about regulation is that they don't understand what the job is. They don't see themselves as "making a thing that people can use," but rather believing that for some insane reason, companies and organizations owe them time, budgets, and resources to make some fucking art. For the record, I have nothing against art. I love art. I'm an artist myself. I'm also a designer. I understand the difference between the two. Design is the solution to a problem, but that problem is never your self-esteem.

When I think back to some of the most innovative stuff that's happened in web design—image compression, responsive design, pattern languages, and video streaming—these things happened not *in spite of* constraints, but *because* of them.

This argument is moot.

Licensing is more often used to pull rank than to serve the public good.

This is absolutely possible inasmuch as every system is prone to corruption. Power corrupts. The ability to license and unlicense others to do their jobs will no doubt attract the weak-willed and corruptible, but it will also attract people who want our profession to rise to new heights. It'll be on us to support the latter while repudiating the former.

Licensing won't be a cure-all by any means. It merely gives us a way to put checks and balances on ourselves that we currently don't have. It's gonna require vigilance and constant refinement. So why go through the hassle? Because I believe we have a lot to gain by giving ourselves control over the quality of our work, certainly more to gain than to lose.

This issue is real.

Licensing will put an undue burden on the poor

Holy shit. This is a very real concern. Of all the concerns I've heard, this is the one that tempts me to toss the whole idea of licensing in the trash. We can't add another burden to the people we need the *most* in this profession. If anything, we should be actively working to remove burdens from their path, rather than adding to those burdens. Any licensing solution needs to take this into account, but if you go back to the previous chapter, you'll see that one of the benefits some of the professional organizations I pointed to are scholarships. That's one possibility. I'm sure we can think of others. I look forward to this discussion.

This argument is real.

Licensing will silo a profession that thrives on generalists

Your family doctor is a generalist and she's licensed. Lawyers range from general practitioners to very specialized practitioners. If anything, this goes the other way. Both of those professions require their members to get a basic general understanding of their fields before they declare a specialization and some, like your family doctor, never do. *Every* doctor, no matter their specialization, can take your blood, diagnose you with a cold or flu, stitch up a wound, and deliver a baby. If anything, licensing can come with a requirement that all designers have a solid foundation of general practices.

This point is moot.

It's impossible

This is like the last runner coming off the blocks complaining that racing conditions are bad. The last runner off the blocks just needs to follow the ass in front of them. Too many professions have managed to license their practitioners for this to be a serious argument. Again, this comes down to the misunderstanding that we're somehow special in nature. We're not. You have a skill that can be taught, and while you may have a natural aptitude for design, it's no different from a lawyer's natural aptitude for the law. We're skilled workers. We're not unique in that aspect. It's easy to license skilled workers.

I love you, but it's time to kill some dreams. For decades, we let other people refer to us as "creatives." It made us feel good. It made us feel special. This was a term coined by marketing agencies in the 50s to refer to all the people in the office who didn't wear suits or vote for Eisenhower. It's not an empowering term, and no, we're not "reclaiming" it. We're burning it with fire. It's a word for which we traded our agency, value, and stakeholdership. We're not creatives, we're designers. We may think and do our work in creative ways, but we're not special in that regard. Everyone else in the office who's worth their salt works in creative ways. Make them call you by your name. That name is designer.

We don't have a universal definition of design

Ask ten designers for a definition of design and you'll get ten different answers and five will be self-serving. "A designer is someone who's amazingly creative and doesn't need to come to requirements meetings, especially if they're early in the morning." Yet when something they design doesn't work, it's not their fault because they're "just doing what they're told" and "shut up, I have rent to pay." Our shifty definition of design has been quite helpful, mainly to us. It allows us to slither and slide toward the things we enjoy doing, while avoiding accountability. To further muddy things up, now people are saying that everyone is a designer. What are we to do, license everyone? That's obviously impractical and stupid.

Let's start by dealing with the "everyone is a designer" issue. First off, it's true. Ish. Everyone in your company impacts design from the people allocating budgets to the people making decisions on timelines to the people allocating resources. If you have two years and a team of twenty-four to design something, it'll come out different than if you have six weeks and a team of three. That's how those things affect design. Someone who gives you great feedback affects design. A developer who engineers a better way to implement something affects the design. So, in this sense, everyone is a designer in that they impact the work.

You are the one who was hired as a designer. That means it all falls on your head. You're the one who has to make the budgets and timelines work. You're the one who has to recognize that good feedback. You're the one who has to take all these suggestions and input and constraints and make something out of it. (Be mindful that "you" is also a plural.)

Lawyers spend their entire lives defining the law. They didn't wait until they had a concrete definition to start organizing their field. They understood it was gonna be a constant battle. For licensing purposes, our job is infinitely easier than defining where design begins and ends. If anything, our lack of a unified definition of design is a reason to license the field, not a reason not to. All we have to do is define where the design stakeholder responsibilities begin and end. That's doable.

DIAPERS FOR PARAKEETS

There's a point in *Design For the Real World* where Papanek just gets fed up with trying to make designers understand how much they're not doing the job they're cashing checks for, loses his shit, stops trying to make rational arguments, and just starts screaming about diapers for parakeets:

> *Through wasting design talent on such trivia as mink-covered toilet seats, chrome-plated marmalade guards for toast, electronic fingernail-polish dryers, and baroque fly-swatters, a whole category of fetish objects for an abundant society has been created. I saw an advertisement extolling the virtues of diapers for parakeets.*

I've reached the diapers for parakeets moment myself several times while writing this book, but never as much as during the topic of licensing. I'll admit to some of that being on me. It's a hard topic, and it's easy for it to take you down a wormhole. Like I freely admitted, I don't have a solution for you but to take a look at the state of our industry, and more importantly, what our industry has done to the state of the world and not to feel some sense of shame scares me! We didn't do our jobs. We were supposed to defend the world against monsters and enshittification! We were the last line of defense against rampant greed. We had it within our power to make things better than they are. All the shit that's out there is out there with our fingerprints all over it. When we look out over the landscape of our complicity, we wonder what filter we should use to take our selfie and whether it goes in our feed or a story. We are making diapers for parakeets. We needed to hold ourselves accountable. We refused to do it. Now society wants to hold us accountable. Our argument is that we're too special to be held accountable. We're not. We're still making diapers for parakeets. Our industry is growing up. It's hurting people, and we're throwing a temper tantrum. Maybe the parakeets aren't the ones needing diapers.

On December 11, 2018, Congress pulled Google CEO Sundar Pichai in for questioning about its algorithm and search ranking, among other things. What could've been a great opportunity to find out about how Google's search algorithm works, and whether it's in fact weighted toward one particular ideology or not (as some members were claiming), instead turned into a Thanksgiving dinner nightmare where all the old Fox News inclined relatives were asking the younger dude for tech support. It was clear the Congressional panel didn't even know what questions to ask, so they resorted to sound bites that would play well to their base. At one point, Texas congressman Louie Gohmert told Pichai, "You run off conservatives; you embrace liberals. It's time Google was not immune and held accountable." (He offered no proof.) But what does it mean to be held accountable? And by whom? By Congress? It became clear during the hearing they wanted no part of that. As Fortune reported:

> While lawmakers generally didn't support more regulation, they did
> call for Google to conduct more internal oversight related to bias and

that, if not, it could suffer some undefined consequences.

In other words, we don't know what you're doing, but whatever it is, you better stop it or else. The problem here is that the tech industry has had an opportunity for internal oversight. It's failed. Time and time again, companies have shown that, "what's good for the world isn't necessarily what's good for Facebook." Or Google. Or Twitter. Or Uber. Or tomorrow's valuation unicorns. At some point, Congress, the majority of whom still print out all of their emails, will have to come in and regulate us.

My favorite moment from that particular hearing came towards the end. Republican congress members barraged Pichai with questions about why the results of their ego searches were always negative. California congressman Ted Lieu cut them off with, "if you want positive search results, do positive things."

As designers, we would do well to heed this particular congressman's words. If we want positive search results, we should do positive things. If we want to reassure the users of our products that they can trust us, we should do positive things.

There's a reason I wrote these last three chapters in this order. Community breeds standards; standards breed accountability; accountability breeds trust; licensure validates that trust. It's a journey. It may be a long journey, but that doesn't mean it's not worth taking.

Do positive things.

Conclusion

In her book, *Read & Riot,* Nadya Tolokonnikova of Pussy Riot writes:

What was in fact blown up on the 8th of November 2016 was the social contract, the paradigm that says you can live comfortably without getting your hands dirty with politics.

That social contract was blown up, in part, by using the tools that you and I built with our own hands. So, to say that designers shouldn't get political isn't just naive, it's revisionist. We were being political when we built those tools. Whether we did it on purpose or through ignorance is irrelevant. We did it. Anyone out there telling you designers need to stop getting political is a fool. These are our chickens coming home to roost, so the very least we can do is clean up the chicken shit. But we owe more than that. We owe the world a better chicken coop.

Joe Strummer told us the future is unwritten. That's mostly true, but not completely. Some chapters are already in the books. Jack Dorsey and Mark Zuckerberg's stories are coming to a close. Our children and their children will read about them. They'll be sidebars, cautionary tales of people who had an opportunity to do good in the world, and didn't have the strength of character to do the right thing. Their stories are written. Yours isn't.

If the lessons in this book seem hard, it's because they are meant to be. If the job I'm asking you to do seems difficult, it's because it is. Hard and difficult aren't the same as impossible. When it comes down to it, all I'm asking you to do is the job you signed up for. Close your eyes for a second. Imagine a world in which Facebook actually vetted the news it was publishing before the 2016 election. Imagine a world in which Twitter didn't work overtime to normalize the alt-right to save its own bottom line. Imagine a world in which the service economy isn't widening the gap between the rich and poor. In short, imagine a world in which we had done our jobs.

Now is not the time for designers to get political. That was yesterday. Now's the time to wake up and fight.

By political, I'm talking about caring who our work is affecting. I'm talking about caring about who it's helping and who it's hurting. I'm talking about who's making design decisions, and who's being left out of them. I'm talking about increasing our definition of design beyond aesthetics and into ramifications. I'm talking about what we're willing to support and what we're willing to lay the tools down for.

I'm talking about taking care of people.

I don't give a good fuck whether you're a Democrat, a Republican, a Tory, a Socialist, a Liberal, a Conservative, a Mason, a Whig, or whether you take your orders directly from L'il Wayne albums played backward. As long as you are a designer, you have a responsibility to make the world better for the rest of humanity. If you are a designer, you are a human being first. It is your job to stop those that would denigrate humanity for their own selfish benefit.

We are the defense against monsters.

This job isn't about helping Nike sell shoes. It's about making sure everyone has shoes.

This job isn't about creating bullhorns for fascists and others who'd use their power to denigrate others. It's about making sure those who are threatened by the inhumane have the better bullhorns.

This job isn't about building tools that hand our data to the corporations of Silicon Valley. It's about building tools to keep that data from them.

How will we pay our rent? Tech workers are some of the highest paid workers on the planet. You're not Jean Valjean. You're not a loaf of bread away from your family dying of hunger. Your argument is invalid.

For too long, we've treated the job as if we were servants. We did what we're told. We followed orders. We didn't ask questions. We may have rolled our eyes once in a while when something didn't seem right, but we did it anyway. We behaved as if we had no say and no agency in how the job was done. We lost control of our labor, our hands, and finally we lost our minds.

Yes, design is political. Because design is labor, and your labor is political. Where you choose to expend your labor is a political act. Who you choose to expend it for is a political act. Who we omit from those solutions is a political act. Finally, how we choose to leverage our collective power is the biggest political act we can take. If we choose to work collectively, we have a ton of power. If we continue to behave like servants, we're not just letting ourselves down, we're letting down everyone whose lives we swore to improve.

We're late to the party. The world is working exactly as we designed it to work, and that's the problem. We're here because we've abdicated our responsibility as a line of defense. We're here because we forgot how much strength we have. It's time to remember.

Wake up and fight.

Further Reading

This book was written on the backs of lots of other books, books that helped me understand design, ethics, the space we work in, our relationship to each other, and how to be a better human being. I'm including them here not just to acknowledge my debt to the people who wrote them, but to inspire you to dig into them as well.

Design for the Real World, *Victor Papanek, 1971*

The best design book you'll ever read. Victor saw all of this before anyone else. When it was published in 1971, it was called "radical" and those were the positive reviews. I call it indispensable. Often available used. Every ten years or so, someone prints a fresh batch.

Brotopia: Breaking Up the Boys' Club of Silicon Valley, *Emily Chang, 2018*

Like the *Hollywood Babylon* of Silicon Valley. If you think I'm making up horror stories in this book, read Brotopia. Emily Chang collected all the receipts.

Broad Band: The Untold Story of the Women Who Made the Internet, *Claire L. Evans, 2018*

If you think men in tech are terrible now (I do), wait until you read about all the shit they did to get women out of a field in which women used to dominate.

So You Wanna Talk About Race, *Ijeoma Oluo, 2018*

When I started reading Ijeoma Oluo's book, I kept thinking, "Oh, this isn't about me," and about halfway through I started saying, "Oh my god, this is totally me." It's a tough read and a good read.

Read & Riot: A Pussy Riot Guide to Activism,
Nadya Tolokonnikova, 2018
I was lucky enough to speak at the same conference with Nadya Tolokonnikova once. She gave a talk about prison reform. It was brutal. It was moving. It was heartfelt, and it was smart. Most of all, it reminded me of being young and wanting to smash the state, and how maybe that wasn't such a bad idea after all.

The Color of Law: A Forgotten History of How Our Government Segregated America, *Richard Rothstein, 2017*
America is racist by design and this book has the blueprints. From tearing down desegregated neighborhoods in the '40s, to building segregated suburbs, to racial qualifications for home loans, to gerrymandering voting districts, it's all being done by design. America didn't fall apart. It was ruined by design.

Twitter and Tear Gas: The Power and Fragility of Networked Protest, *Zeynep Tukecki, 2017*
How modern movements used social networks to communicate with each other and the rest of the world and how those social networks succeeded and failed those movements.

The Jungle, *Upton Sinclair, 1906*
"The Jungle exposed the appalling working conditions in the ~~meat-packing~~ industry. Sinclair's tale of diseased, rotten, and contaminated ~~meat~~ shocked the public and led to new federal ~~food~~ safety laws." Same shit. Different industry.

Thank you

Thank you to everyone who's out there organizing, marching, making lists, making signs, writing chants, and fighting for human decency. You are the helpers. And you are seen.

Thank you to everyone who's ever told a bad boss to go fuck themselves.

Thank you to everyone who's ever told a bad co-worker to sit the fuck back down and shut up.

Thank you to all the young people trying to put the world back together.

Thank you to all the teachers who show up everyday to do their job, and the students who push them to do their best.

Thank you to all the journalists who fight to keep us informed in spite of all the threats against them.

Thank you to all the immigrants who keep striving to maintain their dignity, their strength, and their resolve. I see you. I am one of you. And we will continue to get the job done no matter how much shit they throw at us.

Thank you to every musician, every zine maker, every writer, every street artist who taught me that we don't need to get anyone's permission to get our words, our noise, or our pictures out. Thank you to D Boon for teaching me that punk rock was whatever I wanted it to be.

Thank you to Vivianne Castillo for writing my foreword. The rest of you should take heed, Vivianne is going to rule the world someday. It'll be a better place for it, too.

Thank you to Ani King and Erika Hall for editing my book. Thank you to Amanda Durbin and Mandy Keifetz for proofreading it.

Thank you to David McCreath for the title.

Thank you to Steph Monette, Heather Champ, Derek Powazek, Matt Haughey, Jeff Tidwell, Dian Holton, Dan Sinker, Kate Iselin, Ross Floate, and Gabriel Levine for letting me interview them for this book. Your insight was invaluable.

Thank you to Karen Wickre and Heather Armstrong for helping me navigate the sewer waters of publishing.

Thanks to all the conference organizers who take a chance on letting me on their stage, and to the people who come out to hear me. I hope I never let you down.

Thanks to everyone who keeps me in the air when I'm flying.

Thank you to my wife Erika, who puts up with my moods, my anxiety, my shitty first drafts, and my pacing back and forth around the house. I promise I will never write another book again. (Narrator: He's totally writing another book.)

Thank you to my daughter Chelsea, the bravest among us, for continually teaching me how much I still have to learn, and for filling our lives with joy, kindness, and love. I hope to be as good a writer as you are someday.

Thanks to Annette Rankin for keeping me alive.

Thanks to both my black dogs for giving me enough headspace to do things like this.

Thanks to everyone in my secret Slack group for keeping me grounded and the occasional much-needed laugh.

But mostly, mostly, mostly, thanks to Gritty. When the world was at its darkest, you descended into our lives like a magical agent of chaos riding a wrecking ball of joy. You're the hero we needed.

Endnotes

1   https://www.vox.com/policy-and-politics/2019/3/17/18269617/new-zealand-shooting-mosque-online-extremism-tech

2   https://www.buzzfeed.com/azeenghorayshi/grindr-hiv-status-privacy

3   http://www.pnas.org/content/111/24/8788.full

4   https://www.theverge.com/2018/1/12/16882408/google-racist-gorillas-photo-recognition-algo-rithm-ai

5   https://www.forbes.com/sites/kalevleetaru/2017/05/01/how-facebook-secretly-turned-us-all-in-to-digital-lab-rats/#5ed089ec2223

6   https://www.theguardian.com/world/2018/jan/28/fitness-tracking-app-gives-away-location-of-se-cret-us-army-bases

7   https://www.buzzfeed.com/ryanmac/growth-at-any-cost-top-facebook-executive-defended-data

8   https://theintercept.com/2017/03/02/palantir-provides-the-engine-for-donald-trumps-deporta-tion-machine/

9   https://techcrunch.com/2018/04/11/zuckerberg-doesnt-want-to-talk-about-changing-the-busi-ness-model/

10 From Brotopia, by Emily Chang

11 https://www.theguardian.com/commentisfree/2018/jul/01/smart-home-devices-internet-of-things-domestic-abuse

12 https://www.theguardian.com/technology/2018/jul/19/mark-zuckerberg-holocaust-denial-face-book-remarks-offensive

13 https://www.wsj.com/articles/you-give-apps-sensitive-personal-information-then-they-tell-face-book-11550851636

14 https://www.recode.net/2018/2/8/16989834/twitter-q4-2018-earnings-revenue-jack-dorsey

15 https://www.cnn.com/2017/08/15/politics/trump-charlottesville-delay/index.html

16 https://www.rsph.org.uk/our-work/campaigns/status-of-mind.html

17 https://www.youtube.com/watch?v=gTEDYCkNqns

18 https://www.buzzfeednews.com/article/bensmith/uber-executive-suggests-dig-ging-up-dirt-on-journalists

19 https://www.washingtonpost.com/posteverything/wp/2015/07/23/as-a-black-man-its-hard-to-catch-a-cab-research-shows-even-white-people-know-that/

20 https://www.bbc.com/news/business-34324772

21 https://generalassemb.ly/education/user-experience-design

22 https://www.ncwit.org/resources/women-tech-facts-2016-update

23 https://www.talentinnovation.org/_private/assets/Athena-2-PressRelease-CTI.pdf

24 https://www.fbo.gov/index?s=opportunity&mode=form&id=151d4eaab6927f4e2d6d396d084c23f
   1&tab=core&_cview=1

25 https://www.nytimes.com/2013/05/05/magazine/y-combinator-silicon-valleys-start-up-machine.
   html

26 https://www.vanityfair.com/news/2017/09/north-korea-says-trumps-tweets-are-a-declaration-of-
   war

27 https://news.mongabay.com/2017/10/amazon-deforestation-linked-to-mcdonalds-and-british-re-
   tail-giants/

28 https://www.theguardian.com/lifeandstyle/2019/jan/23/faking-it-how-selfie-dysmorphia-is-driv-
   ing-people-to-seek-surgery

29 https://www.newyorker.com/magazine/2018/09/17/can-mark-zuckerberg-fix-facebook-before-it-
   breaks-democracy

30 https://www.news.com.au/technology/online/social/tinder-has-launched-a-new-feature-that-
   tracks-places-you-visit/news-story/4cc07b09a779fa92c761a1e1fd78dd4c

31 https://techcrunch.com/2014/05/29/philz-coffee-drops-euclid-analytics-over-privacy-concerns/

32 https://www.propublica.org/article/facebook-is-letting-job-advertisers-target-only-men

33 https://www.cdc.gov/measles/vaccination.html

34 https://www.theatlantic.com/health/archive/2015/01/the-new-measles/384738/

35 https://www.cnbc.com/2017/08/09/9-companies-that-cover-100-percent-of-employee-health-in-
   surance-premiums.html

36 https://www.cia.gov/news-information/featured-story-archive/2012-featured-story-archive/Clean-
   edUOSSSimpleSabotage_sm.pdf

37 https://www.vox.com/policy-and-politics/2019/3/4/18249872/oakland-teachers-strike-pay-raise

38 https://www.nytimes.com/2018/11/01/technology/google-walkout-sexual-harassment.html

39 http://nymag.com/intelligencer/2018/11/mark-zuckerberg-gives-defiant-cnn-interview.html

40 https://www.businessinsider.com/mark-zuckerberg-whats-good-for-world-not-necessarily-face-
   book-2018-12

Index

working within the system 10, 47–8, 56, 91–5, 174

About the Author

Mike Monteiro lives with his family in San Francisco. He lives in constant fear of being evicted from their home so it can be rented out to some tech dickhead at four times the price.

Last week his wife, Erika Hall, told him the one thing he wasn't was cynical and that made him happy for a few days.

He's available to speak at your conference, teach your employees how to do their jobs, and write more books.

Colophon

You know what? I'm not even gonna tell you. You focus too much on stuff like this as it is. Focus on bigger things. That was the whole point of this book. Who cares what typeface I used? It's legible enough. Deal with it.